Torture

DATE DUE

Other Books in the Current Controversies Series

Torture

Debra A. Miller, Book Editor

GREENHAVEN PRESS
A part of Gale, Cengage Learning

Detroit • New York • San Francisco • New Haven, Conn • Waterville, Maine • London

Christine Nasso, *Publisher*
Elizabeth Des Chenes, *Managing Editor*

© 2009 Greenhaven Press, a part of Gale, Cengage Learning

Gale and Greenhaven Press are registered trademarks used herein under license.

For more information, contact:
Greenhaven Press
27500 Drake Rd.
Farmington Hills, MI 48331-3535
Or you can visit our Internet site at gale.cengage.com

For product information and technology assistance, contact us at

Gale Customer Support, 1-800-877-4253
For permission to use material from this text or product, submit all requests online at www.cengage.com/permissions

Further permissions questions can be emailed to permissionrequest@cengage.com

Articles in Greenhaven Press anthologies are often edited for length to meet page requirements. In addition, original titles of these works are changed to clearly present the main thesis and to explicitly indicate the author's opinion. Every effort is made to ensure that Greenhaven Press accurately reflects the original intent of the authors. Every effort has been made to trace the owners of copyrighted material.

Cover image copyright Tammy Allen, 2009. Used under license from Shutterstock.com.

LIBRARY OF CONGRESS CATALOGING-IN-PUBLICATION DATA

Torture / Debra A. Miller, book editor.
   p. cm. -- (Current controversies)
   Includes bibliographical references and index.
   ISBN 978-0-7377-4326-5 (hardcover)
   ISBN 978-0-7377-4325-8 (pbk.)
   1. Torture. 2. Torture--United States. I. Miller, Debra A.
   HV8593.T6619 2009
   364.6'7--dc22

                                            2008049217

Printed in the United States of America
1 2 3 4 5 6 7 13 12 11 10 09

Contents

Chapter 1: How Common Is the Use of Torture?

Chapter 2: Is Torture Morally Wrong?

Yes: Torture Is Morally Wrong

Chapter 3: Is Torture an Effective Interrogation Technique?

No: Torture Is Not an Effective Interrogation Technique

Chapter 4: What Should Be the U.S. Policy on Torture?

Foreword

By definition, controversies are "discussions of questions in which opposing opinions clash" (Webster's Twentieth Century Dictionary Unabridged). Few would deny that controversies are a pervasive part of the human condition and exist on virtually every level of human enterprise. Controversies transpire between individuals and among groups, within nations and between nations. Controversies supply the grist necessary for progress by providing challenges and challengers to the status quo. They also create atmospheres where strife and warfare can flourish. A world without controversies would be a peaceful world; but it also would be, by and large, static and prosaic.

The Series' Purpose

The purpose of the Current Controversies series is to explore many of the social, political, and economic controversies dominating the national and international scenes today. Titles selected for inclusion in the series are highly focused and specific. For example, from the larger category of criminal justice, Current Controversies deals with specific topics such as police brutality, gun control, white collar crime, and others. The debates in Current Controversies also are presented in a useful, timeless fashion. Articles and book excerpts included in each title are selected if they contribute valuable, long-range ideas to the overall debate. And wherever possible, current information is enhanced with historical documents and other relevant materials. Thus, while individual titles are current in focus, every effort is made to ensure that they will not become quickly outdated. Books in the Current Controversies series will remain important resources for librarians, teachers, and students for many years.

In addition to keeping the titles focused and specific, great care is taken in the editorial format of each book in the series. Book introductions and chapter prefaces are offered to provide background material for readers. Chapters are organized around several key questions that are answered with diverse opinions representing all points on the political spectrum. Materials in each chapter include opinions in which authors clearly disagree as well as alternative opinions in which authors may agree on a broader issue but disagree on the possible solutions. In this way, the content of each volume in Current Controversies mirrors the mosaic of opinions encountered in society. Readers will quickly realize that there are many viable answers to these complex issues. By questioning each author's conclusions, students and casual readers can begin to develop the critical thinking skills so important to evaluating opinionated material.

Current Controversies is also ideal for controlled research. Each anthology in the series is composed of primary sources taken from a wide gamut of informational categories including periodicals, newspapers, books, U.S. and foreign government documents, and the publications of private and public organizations. Readers will find factual support for reports, debates, and research papers covering all areas of important issues. In addition, an annotated table of contents, an index, a book and periodical bibliography, and a list of organizations to contact are included in each book to expedite further research.

Perhaps more than ever before in history, people are confronted with diverse and contradictory information. During the Persian Gulf War, for example, the public was not only treated to minute-to-minute coverage of the war, it was also inundated with critiques of the coverage and countless analyses of the factors motivating U.S. involvement. Being able to sort through the plethora of opinions accompanying today's major issues, and to draw one's own conclusions, can be a complicated and frustrating struggle. It is the editors' hope that Current Controversies will help readers with this struggle.

Introduction

"Since the terrorist attacks of September 11, 2001, . . . a debate over how to define torture has emerged as a result of former president George W. Bush's efforts to combat the new terrorist threat by pushing the boundaries of what actions constitute torture."

Almost everyone agrees that certain actions constitute torture. These actions would include physical assault, beatings, use of electric shock, employment of mind-altering drugs, rape, and various other behaviors that would obviously cause great pain and harm to the bodies and minds of human beings. Trying to agree on a single legal definition of torture, however, has sometimes proved problematic for the world's governments.

International agreements on the subject have used various definitions. The 1948 Universal Declaration of Human Rights states that "no one shall be subjected to torture or to cruel, inhuman, or degrading treatment." Article 17 of the Third Geneva Convention (1949), which addresses the treatment of prisoners of war, asserts that "no physical or mental torture, nor any other form of coercion, may be inflicted on prisoners of war," and requires that "persons taking no active part in the hostilities . . . shall in all circumstances be treated humanely." Most recently, the 1985 United Nations (UN) Convention Against Torture defines torture broadly as:

Any act by which severe pain or suffering, whether physical or mental, is intentionally inflicted on a person for such purposes as obtaining from him or a third person information or a confession, punishing him for an act he or a third person has committed or is suspected of having committed, or intimidating or coercing him or a third person, or for any reason based on discrimination of any kind, when such pain or suffering is inflicted by or at the instigation of or with the consent or acquiescence of a public official or other person acting in an official capacity.

Today, most legal definitions of torture follow this 1985 definition, emphasizing that torture is any act that intentionally inflicts severe pain or suffering, whether physical or mental, when executed to serve a state purpose other than punishment, such as a need to gather intelligence information or intimidate government dissenters.

The United States has historically incorporated these international definitions into its military manuals. The 1992 U.S. Army Field Manual, for example, instructs soldiers that both the Geneva Conventions and U.S. policy prohibit acts of violence or intimidation, including physical or mental torture, threats, or insults as a means of interrogation. Since the terrorist attacks of September 11, 2001, however, a debate over how to define torture has emerged as a result of former president George W. Bush's efforts to combat the new terrorist threat by pushing the boundaries of what actions constitute torture.

In 2002, for example, the Justice Department's Office of Legal Counsel issued a memo that asserted that coercive interrogations constitute torture only if they intentionally caused suffering "equivalent in intensity to the pain accompanying serious physical injury, such as organ failure, impairment of bodily function, or even death." That memo was rescinded in 2004, but the administration apparently continued to authorize or otherwise permit highly coercive interrogation techniques, claiming that they did not rise to the level of torture. Administration officials have referred to these as "enhanced" interrogation techniques, but critics refer to them as "torture lite."

In February 2005, for example, the Justice Department issued a secret memorandum on the subject of torture, providing explicit authorization for government interrogators to use a variety of painful physical and psychological tactics against terrorist suspects, including head-slapping, frigid temperatures, and waterboarding (a technique designed to make a victim feel as if he or she is drowning). Other interrogation techniques discovered to have been used in U.S. detention facilities as part of the war on terror were not publicly acknowledged or explicitly approved, even though high-level administration figures reportedly were made aware of them.

These measures included prolonged standing, removal of detainees' clothing, sensory deprivation, hooding (covering prisoners' heads), prolonged interrogations, use of dogs to instill fear, forced shaving of beards, grabbing, poking, pushing, and sleep manipulation and deprivation. Interrogators also used religious and sexual humiliation, prolonged shackling, exposure to heat, food or toilet deprivation, and mock or threatened executions. According to reports, these techniques were used frequently in Central Intelligence Agency interrogations; at detention facilities in Guantánamo Bay, Cuba; and in U.S. detention facilities in Iraq, such as the prison at Abu Ghraib, which became famous for photos showing naked prisoners in various humiliating positions. The administration also was heavily criticized for sending terrorist suspects to foreign countries that are known to use torture.

Despite these criticisms, however, former President Bush maintained throughout the post-9/11 period that the United States has complied with the international prohibition against torture because its "enhanced" interrogation techniques do not constitute torture. The president firmly believes that enhanced interrogation techniques are necessary to obtain much-needed intelligence information in the war on terror. The administration's position and its flexibility in defining torture have raised difficult questions about U.S. policies on torture, how narrowly torture can be defined by the executive branch, and whether it is ever appropriate for the government to employ any type of torture techniques against terrorist suspects.

The authors of the viewpoints included in *Current Controversies: Torture* address many of the most compelling issues in the torture debate. These issues include whether torture is common in today's world, whether it is moral, whether it is an effective interrogation technique, and what should be the U.S. policy on torture in the new world of international terrorism.

CHAPTER 1

How Common Is the Use of Torture?

Chapter Preface

Torture, by definition, typically involves the intentional infliction of either physical or psychological pain. Often, the torture continues over long periods of time—days, weeks, or months. Sometimes, the torture is exceptionally cruel. As a result, even after the torture has ended, most victims experience medical and psychological aftereffects of varying degrees. Many victims are scarred for life.

The consequences of torture depend, to a large extent, on the nature and duration of the torture. Physical torture can range from simple beatings to more severe physical abuse, such as cigarette burns, simulated drowning or choking, restraints such as handcuffing or shackling, pulled or broken teeth, extreme heat or cold, or stress positions that cause numbness or dislocate bones and joints. In other cases, victims may be prodded on sensitive parts of the body with electric shock devices, partially suffocated, drugged, or subjected to forced labor or exercise. Perhaps the worst kinds of physical torture, however, are actions that cause permanent disfiguration, mutilation, or disability. These severe types of torture include severe beatings; the chopping off of ears, noses, or fingers; or the throwing of acids onto faces or other parts of the body. The withholding of medical care often exacerbates the effects of these various physical abuses.

Psychological torture can be just as damaging. Victims might be deprived of basic needs (such as food, water, sleep, toilet facilities, or clothing), prevented from sleeping, or kept isolated for long periods of time. They may be humiliated in various ways, deprived of sensory input by the use of blindfolds or hoods, forced to listen to extremely loud noise that damages hearing, forced to watch or perform degrading acts that cause fear and anguish, or threatened with harm to themselves or their families. Other forms of mental torture include prolonged aggressive questioning, attempts to confuse the victim or telling the victim false stories about tragedies affecting their friends or families, and the use of sexual torture techniques that range from verbal abuse to rape or sexual assault.

The results of torture run the gamut from mild to severe and can manifest in physical or psychological trauma, or both. Physical consequences can include chronic pain in affected parts of the body; hemorrhages or infections caused by physical damage to internal organs or body cavities; and painful and permanent scars, mutilation, or disfiguration. Psychological consequences often can be seen in psychiatric conditions such as moodiness, anxiety, depression, panic attacks, phobias, post-traumatic stress disorders, and suicidal tendencies. Many victims of torture also suffer from overwhelming feelings of powerlessness, problems with concentration, sleeplessness, frequent nightmares, and sexual impotence or dysfunction. These conditions in turn often make it difficult for the victim to engage in normal social activities, obtain jobs or remain employed, or otherwise live a normal or productive life.

The advocacy group Physicians for Human Rights recently documented many typical post-torture medical effects in a 2008 report entitled *Broken Laws, Broken Lives: Medical Evidence of Torture by U.S. Personnel and Its Impact.* The group interviewed, examined, and tested eleven former detainees who were held in U.S. custody overseas as part of the war on terror. The study found that these detainees were subjected to various types of physical and mental torture, including isolation, humiliation, sleep deprivation, extreme temperatures, stress positions, hooding, forced nakedness, severe humiliation, and sensory deprivation or bombardment. Former detainees also complained of physical beatings and sexual assaults. The group found that the medical consequences of these types of torture were severe, including physical conditions such as permanent internal and external scarring; chronic headaches; and numbness and pain in limbs, joints, back, muscles, and ligaments. Psychological symptoms ranged from chest pain and severe anxiety to chronic sleeplessness, depression, post-traumatic stress disorder, unresolved anger, and suicidal thoughts.

And experts say the pain and anxiety of torture is not always limited to the immediate victim. Spouses and families of the victim also often suffer great anguish, both while the victim is being detained and after he or she is released in a broken state. In fact, in situations where detention and torture are common, even entire communities can sometimes be affected, becoming more fearful and less contented places to live. The pain of torture appears to ripple outward long after the actual acts of torture have ended.

The viewpoints in this chapter consider and discuss how common torture is in our modern world and provide specific examples of where it is occurring.

Torture Is a Worldwide Problem

Human Rights Watch

Human Rights Watch is an independent nongovernmental organization dedicated to protecting the human rights of people around the world.

Many countries continue to brutalize detainees or suspects. Some governments justify such abuses as inevitable in the global war on terrorism. Others use the excuse of more local enemies. But in any context, such abuses have terrible long-term consequences, destroy the lives of detainees, dehumanize interrogators, and are absolutely prohibited by universally agreed-upon standards.

China

Torture is common in China's criminal justice system. Recent HRW [Human Rights Watch, an anti-torture organization] research suggests that abuses are particularly likely in Tibet and Xinjiang [a Chinese province]. In Tibet, authorities have subjected religious figures and activists to mistreatment in detention.

In Xinjiang, populated mostly by Muslim Uighurs, China has cracked down on religious practitioners and activists and subjected them to abuse in prisons and "re-education through labor" camps—some have also been executed. Detainees have reported beatings with shackles, electric shocks, and being kicked to the point of unconsciousness.

Egypt

Authorities in Egypt use torture on a wide scale. Suspected Islamist militants have borne the brunt of these practices, but the impunity enjoyed by the State Security Investigations (SSI)

Human Rights Watch, "Torture Worldwide," *Human Rights News*, April 27, 2005. www.hrw.org. Copyright © 2005, Human Rights Watch. Reproduced by permission.

arm of the Ministry of Interior has helped to foster a culture of brutality in ordinary police work as well. The government-appointed National Council for Human Rights, in its first annual report, published belatedly in April 2005, acknowledged that torture is part of "normal investigative practice" in Egypt. . . .

Despite Egypt's terrible record of torture and ill-treatment, governments in the region and in the West, including the United States, have "rendered" wanted suspects to Cairo and into the hands of the SSI, in clear violation of the principle of *non-refoulement* [a principle of international refugee law that prohibits returning individuals to countries or territories where their freedom or lives would be threatened]. One of these persons was Mamdouh Habib, an Australian citizen of Egyptian origin captured in Pakistan in October 2001 and transferred by the United States to Egyptian custody for six months and then to Guantanamo Bay. He was released from there without charge in January 2005. While he was in Egypt, according to a court affidavit filed by his U.S. lawyer, "he was subjected to unspeakable brutality," including severe beatings for hours at a time and electric shock treatment of "ingenious cruelty." . . .

Torture and ill-treatment in detention, including indefinite solitary confinement, are routinely used to punish dissidents in Iran.

The rendition of persons to countries that practice torture has been especially problematic among the member states of the Arab League. Of the fifty-six persons known to have been rendered to Egypt over the past decade, thirty-two have been sent there by neighboring Arab countries. In a number of cases, these renditions have involved "swaps" for persons wanted by the sending country, such as Yemen and Libya, where torture is also practiced. The Arab Convention for the

Suppression of Terrorism, which has provided the legal framework for such renditions since it came into effect in April 1998, assumes that such decisions remain in the hands of the executive branches of the governments concerned, with no meaningful role for judicial review or attention to due process concerns in approving extradition requests. Nowhere does the Convention affirm the prohibition against refoulement: indeed, it appears intended to facilitate transfers of persons by short-circuiting torture concerns.

Indonesia

Indonesian security forces in the province of Aceh have systematically tortured detainees suspected of supporting the armed separatist Free Aceh Movement. These prisoners' confessions have routinely served as the basis for convictions in proceedings that fail to meet fair trial standards. Interviewees told Human Rights Watch of routine beatings and threats of beatings, cigarette burnings, and the use of electro-shock at the hands of the police and the military. Several prisoners showed Human Rights Watch scars from such torture.

Iran

Torture and ill-treatment in detention, including indefinite solitary confinement, are routinely used to punish dissidents in Iran. Torture is often carried out in illegal and secret prisons and interrogation centers run by intelligence services, and has been used particularly against those imprisoned for peaceful expression of their political views.

The use of prolonged solitary confinement, often in small basement cells, has been designed to break the will of those detained in order to coerce confessions and provide information regarding associates. Combined with denial of access to counsel and videotaped confessions, prolonged solitary confinement creates an environment in which prisoners have nowhere to turn in order to seek redress for their treatment in detention. Severe physical torture is also used, especially against student activists and others who do not enjoy the high public profile of older dissident intellectuals and writers.

Torture and ill-treatment of security suspects in Iraq has not been confined to U.S.-run detention sites there.

Iraq

Torture and ill-treatment of security suspects in Iraq has not been confined to U.S.-run detention sites there. Human Rights Watch investigations, published in January 2005, found that the Iraqi authorities, in particular the Ministry of Interior, practiced torture and ill-treatment of detainees, denial of access by families and lawyers to detainees, improper treatment of detained children, and abysmal conditions in pre-trial detention facilities. Persons tortured or mistreated have inadequate access to health care and no realistic avenue for legal redress. With rare exception, the Iraqi authorities have failed to investigate and punish officials responsible for violations. International police advisers, primarily U.S. citizens funded by the United States, have turned a blind eye to these rampant abuses.

Between July and October 2004, Human Rights Watch interviewed ninety former and current detainees, of whom seventy-two alleged they had been tortured or ill-treated in detention. Among them were national security suspects, including insurgents, and suspected common criminals accused of serious offenses including terrorism, abduction, money laundering, drug trafficking and acts of sabotage. Methods of torture cited by detainees, principally at the hands of the Ministry of Interior's specialized police agencies, included: routine beatings to the body using a variety of implements such as cables, hosepipes and metal rods; kicking, slapping and punching; prolonged suspension from the wrists with the hands tied behind the back; electric shocks to sensitive parts of the body, including the earlobes and genitals; and being kept blind-folded and/or handcuffed continuously for several days. In several of the cases investigated by Human Rights Watch, de-tainees suffered what may be permanent physical disability.

Abusive interrogation techniques continue to be practiced in Israel.

Many detainees reported that police interrogators made them sign statements without being informed of the content or having the opportunity to read them beforehand. They fre-quently reported that they were forced to sign or fingerprint such statements while blindfolded, often at the end of interro-gation sessions during which they were physically abused. Of-ficials at detention facilities routinely denied relatives and de-fense counsel access to detainees.

Israel

Abusive interrogation techniques continue to be practiced in Israel. The Supreme Court there ruled in September 1999 that six frequently used practices of the Israeli Security Agency (then known as the General Security Service, or GSS) violated existing laws. These included beatings, prolonged sleep depri-vation, violent shaking, and prolonged painful positioning. There appears to be agreement among Israeli human rights activists and defense lawyers that these techniques are used less frequently, but have been replaced by techniques that are extremely stressful psychologically, including: greater isolation for longer periods; denial of access to lawyers and family members for extended periods; prolonged interrogation ses-sions; use of collaborators to threaten detainees; and threats to family members.

The Supreme Court ruling also permits the security agency to claim the "necessity defense" in cases where "exceptional in-terrogation means" are allegedly needed, as in so-called "ticking bomb" cases. The Israeli daily [newspaper] *Ha'aretz* reported in July 2002 that the GSS had up to that point employed "exceptional interrogation means" against ninety Palestinians. The readiness of the Attorney General to grant "necessity defense" requests, along with the fact that since 1999 no Israeli Security Agency or GSS officer has faced criminal or disciplinary charges for acts of torture or ill-treatment, appears to have led to an erosion of the restraints initially imposed by the 1999 ruling.

In addition, physical violence—or the threat of it—is often present in the treatment of detainees. Most former detainees interviewed by Human Rights Watch in 2004 described physical abuse at the time of their arrest and transfer to Israeli detention or interrogation centers.

In North Korea, which suffers one of the world's most repressive governments, prisoners are routinely subjected to forced labor, torture and other mistreatment.

Malaysia

Malaysia has rounded up numerous detainees under its Internal Security Act [ISA], a draconian law that permits the government to detain individuals without charge or trial, denying them even the most basic due process rights. The ISA allows the government to hold detainees for two years after arrest, and then renew this period indefinitely without meaningful judicial approval or scrutiny. In a 2004 Human Rights Watch report, detainees held under the ISA reported that they had been mistreated, subjected to sexual humiliation, and slapped and kicked. All were held incommunicado for several weeks after they were first detained. Family members report that detainees showed signs of more extensive physical abuse when they first were able to meet with them.

Morocco

Morocco has been no exception to the global backsliding in the protection of civil liberties and basic freedoms in the name of counter-terrorism. Recent credible reports of torture and mistreatment of suspects, and the denial of the right to a fair trial, suggest that the broader freedoms Moroccans have enjoyed during the last decade and-a-half can be reversed. . . .

Nepal

Torture and ill-treatment in custody are prevalent throughout Nepal, which is caught in an increasingly brutal nine-year civil war between rebels of the Communist Party of Nepal . . . and government security forces. During the course of the war, the number of enforced disappearances—cases in which people are taken into custody and authorities then deny all responsibility or knowledge of their fate or whereabouts—has reached crisis proportions. . . .

Nigeria

Torture and ill-treatment of criminal suspects in police custody is systematic and routine in Nigeria, with a strong correlation between the severity of the ill-treatment inflicted and the severity of the alleged offense. As a result, armed robbery and murder suspects are generally the most seriously abused and suffer the harshest treatment in detention. . . .

Torture is routinely used in Pakistan by civilian law enforcement agencies, military personnel, and intelligence agencies.

North Korea

In North Korea, which suffers one of the world's most repressive governments, prisoners are routinely subjected to forced labor, torture and other mistreatment. Despite repeated resolutions by the U.N. Human Rights Commission condemning its human rights record, North Korea has largely shunned dialogue with U.N. experts on human rights, including the special rapporteur on human rights in North Korea, Vitit Muntarbhorn.

Pakistan

Torture is routinely used in Pakistan by civilian law enforcement agencies, military personnel, and intelligence agencies. While acts of torture by the police are generally aimed at producing confessions during the course of criminal investigations, torture by military agencies primarily serves to frighten a victim into changing his political stance or loyalties or at the very least to stop him from being critical of the military authorities. Suspects are often whipped to the point of bleeding, severely beaten, and made to stay in painful stress positions. A July 2004 Human Rights Watch report focuses on abuses against farming families in the Punjab, including testimony about killings and torture by paramilitary forces.

Russia's federal forces have detained and "disappeared" thousands of Chechens . . . and tortured them in custody to obtain confessions and information.

Russia

Russia considers its military and policing action in Chechnya to be a counterterrorism operation. Now in its sixth year [as of 2005], the conflict has created a dire human rights crisis. Chechen fighters have committed unspeakable acts of terrorism in Chechnya and in other parts of Russia.

Russia's federal forces have detained and "disappeared" thousands of Chechens whom they suspect of involvement with rebel forces and tortured them in custody to obtain confessions and information.

By carrying out forced disappearances, federal forces in Chechnya attempt to conceal the torture and summary execution of those in their custody, and therefore benefit from impunity for such crimes. "Disappearances" in Chechnya are so widespread and systematic that they constitute crimes against humanity; by some estimates between 3,000 and 5,000 have "disappeared" since 1999. . . .

Syria has a long-established record of torture.

Syria

Syria has a long-established record of torture. The case of Maher Arar, a Canadian of Syrian origin who was detained in 2002 by U.S. authorities in New York's Kennedy Airport while he was in transit to Montreal, is relatively well known. Arar was detained in the New York area for approximately two weeks before he was sent, over his strenuous objections, not to Canada but to Syria. Arar has publicly provided detailed accounts of the torture he says he was subjected to while under interrogation in Syrian custody. He was eventually freed and has returned to Canada, and has brought suits against the United States and Canadian governments for their roles in rendering him into the hands of Syrian torturers. . . .

Turkey

Torture remains common in Turkey today. While the government has declared "zero tolerance" for torture and introduced important reforms in the past five years that have significantly reduced the frequency and severity of torture, ill-treatment persists because police and gendarmes (soldiers who police rural areas) in some areas ignore the new safeguards. Due to poor supervision of police stations, certain police units deny or delay detainees access to a lawyer, fail to inform families that their relatives have been detained, attempt to suppress or influence medical reports which record ill-treatment, and still do not reliably apply special protections for child detainees. . . .

Uganda

The use of torture as a tool of interrogation has featured prominently in escalating human rights violations by Ugandan security and military forces since 2001. Official and ad hoc military, security and intelligence agencies of the Ugandan government have illegally detained and tortured suspects, seeking to force confessions of links to past political opponents or current rebel groups. . . .

Uzbekistan

Uzbekistan has a long history of torture. Since the mid-1990's the Uzbek government has arrested thousands of people on charges of Islamic "fundamentalism" or "extremism," handing down prison sentences to most ranging from 5 to 20 years.

Both Civilized and Less Civilized Countries Use Torture Techniques

Lisa Hajjar

Lisa Hajjar teaches in the Law and Society Program at the University of California at Santa Barbara, is a published author, and serves on the editorial committee of Middle East Report, *a publication that provides information and analysis of Middle East politics and culture.*

The public exposure of torture of Iraqi detainees by US soldiers, working in interrogation wings run by military intelligence and American "security contractors," at Abu Ghraib prison outside of Baghdad—as well as allegations of torture of other Iraqis by British soldiers—are headline news. The shocking revelations and photographs provide stark proof that torture is not a relic of "our past." Nor does torture provide a meaningful geographical or cultural demarcation between "civilized" and "uncivilized" societies.

Implicatory Denial

The fact is that, today, people are being tortured in two-thirds of the world's countries. Yet if one were to accept the rhetoric of the world's states at face value, there is no torture in the world. No torturing regime defends or even acknowledges its own torture as torture. Stanley Cohen, author of *States of Denial*, identifies three common forms of denial of torture and other atrocities. "Literal denial" is when a state accused of torture responds by saying that nothing happened and that those who claim something happened are liars or "enemies of the state." "Interpretative denial" is when a state refutes allegations by saying that what happened is not torture but "something else"—like "moderate physical pressure" or "stress and duress." "Implicatory denial"—that is, denial by implicating others—occurs when a state acknowledges torture but blames it on "aberrant agents," claiming that rogue elements have breached official norms and policies. Official US responses to the Abu Ghraib prison photos are a classic example of implicatory denial. . . .

Torture must be practiced in secret and denied in public because, in the mid-twentieth century, torture became an international crime.

Denial of torture is articulated in many ways, but all states deny it for the same reason. Torture must be practiced in secret and denied in public because, in the mid-twentieth century, torture became an international crime. Irrespective of what penalties the arrested soldiers may face under the Uniform Code of Military Justice, the pictures from Abu Ghraib—whose authenticity no one has denied—document offenses of an especially heinous kind. . . .

Torture and Terror

If torture is so strongly prohibited, and denied by all states because it is fundamentally illegitimate, then why is it so common in today's world? While states torture people for numerous reasons, one common reason invoked by many states is that they claim to be engaged in conflicts with "terrorists."

Terrorism is a broad and flexible concept, and there is no clear, internationally accepted definition. It is used, variously, to describe certain kinds of actions, including attacks on civilians, hijackings, organized resistance or repression, and to identify certain types of actors. In US national security discourse, the term terrorism typically is used to refer to non-state actors or organizations engaged in attacks or struggles against the state, emphasizing but not necessarily limited to violence, to which the state responds with "counter-terrorism."

Terrorism is not a figment of the politically paranoid imagination. The September 11, 2001 attacks were indisputably terrorist attacks, and al-Qaeda operates as a terrorist organization. Any and every instance of deliberately targeting civilians or civilian infrastructures as a tactic in the furtherance of some cause, whatever the political or ideological motivation and whomever the targeting agents, is terroristic. If the deliberate targeting of civilians constitutes terrorism, then we must acknowledge that states can be as culpable as non-state groups. However, as Richard Falk explains [in *The Great Terror War*, 2002]:

> With the help of the influential media, the state over time has waged and largely won the battle of definitions by exempting its own violence against civilians from being treated and perceived as "terrorism." Instead, such violence was generally discussed as "uses of force," "retaliation," "self-defense" and "security measures."

Around the world, some of the most egregious human rights violations have been perpetrated by states in the name of counter-terrorism.

National security is a legitimate interest of any state, and states have a responsibility to provide for the security of their citizens. But the tendency to characterize and treat all "enemies" as "terrorists" or "terrorist sympathizers" contributes to the delineation between "legitimate" and "illegitimate" communities, leaving the latter vulnerable to state violence, and enabling the state to justify that violence as a necessary reaction to terror. Pointing out the limits and obfuscations of national security discourse is not an apologia for terrorism.

Rather, it is an effort to understand, evaluate and criticize violence in a manner that is not glazed by partisan or statist ideology.

Around the world, some of the most egregious human rights violations have been perpetrated by states in the name of counter-terrorism. Terrorism is, by definition, a violation of human rights. Michael Ignatieff, director of the Carr Center of Human Rights Policy at Harvard, writes:

> The two terms—human rights and terror—look like a simple antithesis: human rights good, terror bad. [But] the antithesis is not so simple. Of course, human rights and terror stand opposed to each other. Terrorist acts violate the right to life, along with many other rights. But equally, human rights—notably the right to self-determination—have constituted major justification for the resort to violence, including acts of terror. . . .

Ignatieff correctly points out that it is not international human rights law—which is inherently pacifist—but rather, international humanitarian law that obtains in any war, including a war on terrorism. The Geneva Conventions, which compose the main body of international humanitarian laws [against torture], are agnostic about the causes of war or the justness of the aims of adversaries. Rather, they govern what is legally permissible in war. Their aim is to minimize suffering and destruction, and to . . . [prohibit torture]. Even in war, the right not to be tortured is absolutely non-derogable [not subject to suspension by states in times of emergency], and the use of torture in the context of conflict can constitute a war crime.

Since September 11, the [George W.] Bush administration has articulated positions and pursued policies that blatantly contravene the Geneva Conventions, on the grounds that terrorists do not deserve legal rights and protections. These policies include the invention of a category, "unlawful combatants," that does not exist in international law. These unlawful combatants are being held incommunicado, at Guantánamo Bay and other locations, and subjected to years of interrogation with no judicial oversight, no public accountability and virtually no visitation by representatives of the International Committee of the Red Cross. Although the US government claims that no torture is used in the interrogation of these detainees, these clandestine and extralegal conditions are an invitation for abuse. The Abu Ghraib images are a piece of hard evidence indicating that the US has joined the list of countries—Egypt, Israel, Uzbekistan—that are fighting wars on terrorism partly through the use of torture.

Still, because torture is illegal, it remains necessary for states to deny torture, even the torture of terrorists. In the US, the terrorist attacks of September 11 have raised for debate several vexing and related questions: Should "terrorists" have a right not to be tortured? Is torture a necessary and effective tactic in the fight against terrorism? If so, why deny torture? . . .

"Stress and Duress"

On December 26, 2002, [staff writers] Dana Priest and Barton Gellman published a lengthy story in the *Washington Post* revealing that US security agents were utilizing "stress and duress" tactics in the interrogation of people captured in Afghanistan and elsewhere. The tactics they described are identical to Israeli "moderate physical pressure." Priest and Gellman wrote that: "Those who refuse to cooperate inside this secret CIA [Central Intelligence Agency] interrogation center [at the Bagram air base in Afghanistan] are sometimes kept standing or kneeling for hours, in black hoods or spray-painted goggles, according to intelligence specialists familiar with CIA interrogation methods. At times, they are held in awkward, painful positions and deprived of sleep with a 24-hour bombardment of lights—subject to what are known as 'stress and duress' techniques."

Priest and Gellman also reported that detainees who could not be broken by the "restrained" stress and duress tactics might be given mind-altering drugs or "turned over— 'rendered,' in official parlance—to foreign intelligence services whose practice of torture has been documented by the US government and human rights organizations." They continued, "While the US government publicly denounces the use of torture, each of the current national security officials interviewed for this article defended the use of violence against captives as just and necessary. They expressed confidence that the American public would back their view. The CIA . . . declined to comment." . . .

This *Washington Post* story dramatically altered both what is known about American interrogation and how torture is talked about in the US. Human rights advocates assailed official admissions of "stress and duress" as defenses of torture. On January 11, 2003, in a letter to the *Washington Post*, two former Justice Department officials who served under Presidents Ronald Reagan and George Bush . . . [argued] that "stress and duress" is not torture. "Indeed," they retorted to the human rights advocates, "to say these practices do [constitute torture] ultimately trivializes the torture that does take place in so many areas of the world." So far, the pictures of grinning American soldiers forcing nude Iraqis into sexual positions seem to have dimmed the vigor of this particular defense for the "stress and duress" at Abu Ghraib. However, an ex-US Army interrogation instructor named Tony Robinson, appearing on the *Fox News Channel*'s "Hannity and Colmes" show on April 30 [2004], did say of the pictures that "frat hazing is worse than this."

More to the point, the use of tactics by US officials that arguably constitute torture, and the rendering of prisoners to states with well-established records of torture—including Jordan, Egypt, Syria, Morocco, Pakistan and the Philippines— illuminate the conundrum of what to do about terrorism.

Priest and Gellman recounted the testimony of Cofer Black, former head of the CIA Counterterrorist Center, before Congress on September 26, 2002, to the effect that the CIA and other security agencies need "operational flexibility," and therefore cannot be held to the "old" standards. Black said, "There was 'before' 9/11, and there was 'after' 9/11. After 9/11 the gloves come off."

Tale of Two Clichés

Taking the gloves off in interrogation is a thinly veiled reference to torture, but calling torture "stress and duress" or "abuse" is the homage paid to the still current imperative of denial. The presumptions that torture is both necessary and effective, and the implications of breaking the torture taboo by legalizing torture are shaping debates in the US. This debate circles around two clichés: the slippery slope and the lesser evil. . . .

If torture is practiced by agents of a state that claims to be a democracy, then "we the people" are responsible for torture.

[Supporters of] the slippery slope [view] argue that no cause or crisis justifies the erosion of the absolute prohibition against torture. Variations on this theme include: there is no such thing as just a "little torture," once you start torturing "terrorists" you open the door to torturing anyone in the future and using torture makes you no better than your enemy. Defenders of the lesser evil argue that the absolute prohibition on torture is immoral if it ties the hands of security agents from finding that "ticking bomb" and saving innocent lives. On *CNN*'s "Crossfire," conservative commentator Tucker Carlson said, "Torture is bad. [But] some things are worse. And under some circumstances, it may be the lesser of two evils. Because some evils are pretty evil." . . .

No Room for Mistakes

The slippery slopers present a valuable and worthy defense of taking the moral and legal high road. Those who invoke the slippery slope tend to focus on the tortured and worry—with good cause, as the Abu Ghraib photos have shown—that they are defenseless and susceptible to abuse in custody. But making slippery slope arguments against torture to a public gripped by fear of "evildoers" and willing to sacrifice the rights of "enemies" is not an effective rebuttal to advocates of torture as a lesser evil.

If torture is legitimized and legalized in the future, it is not "the terrorists" who will lose but "the humans."

Those who invoke the lesser evil tend to focus on the public that is vulnerable to terrorism and violence. Their arguments have appeal because many people are willing to accept the legitimacy of torturing terrorists as necessary and effective. Much of the public is willing to trust that government agents empowered to decide whom to torture are capable of discerning real from imagined threats, and restricting torture to the former. But at least 22 Guantánamo Bay detainees—people described as "the worst of the worst" by [former U.S. Secretary of Defense Donald] Rumsfeld—have been released, an implicit acknowledgement that their very detention in a place where torture is likely being used had been a mistake. On May 5 [2004], the *New York Times* published an interview with an Iraqi advancing a credible claim to be the man infamously pictured naked and hooded in Abu Ghraib prison, a female soldier pointing jokingly at his genitalia—was the torture that he is now compelled to relive also a "mistake"? Without effective oversight by a judicial body, the public cannot know or trust that other such "mistakes" will not be made. When it comes to torture, there is no room for a mistake.

Naturally, it is important to focus both on the tortured and on the vulnerable public, but the case of Abu Ghraib shows that it is most important to focus on the torturers. They are representatives of the public they serve. If torture is practiced by agents of a state that claims to be a democracy, then "we the people" are responsible for torture. Citizens of a democracy cannot or at least should not be comforted by blaming a few "aberrant agents" if torture is systemic and routine. Those citizens cannot or should not be quiescent as democratic values and laws are being trampled in a panic. "We the people" are responsible for stopping, protesting and preventing torture.

Keeping torture illegal and struggling to enforce the prohibition are the front lines, quite literally, of a global battle to defend the one core right that all human beings can claim. If torture is legitimized and legalized in the future, it is not "the terrorists" who will lose but "the humans." Should proponents of torture as a lesser evil succeed in regaining legitimacy for the execrable practice, there would be no better words than [British author] George Orwell's from [the book] *1984*: "If you want a picture of the future, imagine a boot stamping on a human face—forever."

Torture Continues to Be a Problem in Asia

Basil Fernando

Basil Fernando is a Sri Lankan human rights lawyer, author, and director of the Asian Human Rights Commission based in Hong Kong.

For over a decade now human rights organizations have extensively documented the practice of torture in many Asian countries. It can be said that—except perhaps for South Korea now and Hong Kong—in almost all other countries torture is routinely practiced as a normal method of investigating crimes.

Police Use of Torture

From petty crimes such as theft to more serious ones such as those under anti-terrorism laws, the basic method by which police seek the "truth" is by torture. Even despite the fact that confessions are not admissible in law, the police and other agencies resort to torture because it is part of the accepted mode of dealing with crime.

Permissiveness toward torture is related to the political system and the nature of policing under a particular system. For example, in a place like Hong Kong, where it is a matter of policy to maintain a rule-of-law system and control corruption, there is hardly any permissiveness toward the use of torture, although there are infrequent reports of the use of pressure on suspects.

However, in most parts of Asia there are still no decisive methods for the control of corruption. A consequence of this is that the police themselves are very much part of the entrenched system of corruption. Every attempt to modernize the policing system threatens the tolerance of corruption.

For this reason no major efforts are made to modernize the policing systems, which continue to rely on primitive techniques in dealing with crime. The most primitive and culturally entrenched tradition coming down from various types of feudal cultures in Asia is torture.

Educating the police about human rights and giving them technical assistance, as are often done by developed countries, have not proved effective in reforming policing systems and eliminating torture. What is required is a comprehensive study that can reveal the historical development of the policing system in each country and the various reasons for the justification of torture.

The theory . . . that information must be obtained quickly from suspects to prevent terror plots . . . has been used to justify the widespread use of torture.

Mere legal condemnation of torture, or declarations at international bodies demanding that this practice be abandoned, cannot resolve this issue, which affects ordinary citizens all the time. It must be understood from its roots.

Some of the narratives about the practice of torture are so shocking that in present-day developed democracies they may not even be considered credible. For example, people may not believe that innocent citizens, mostly from poor backgrounds, can be arrested and tortured to force them to confess to crimes they have not committed, simply because the officers are under pressure to produce a substitute criminal for a crime they are unable to solve.

However, extensive documentation by human rights groups has revealed that this type of practice is very common in countries like Bangladesh, the Philippines, Sri Lanka, Nepal, India, Burma and several other places. The deeper we go into the issue of torture, the more we understand that there are fundamental problems affecting the rule of law as well as democracy in these countries.

Terrorism and Torture

The real or imagined need for anti-terrorism laws has had a negative effect on attempts to eliminate torture in the Asian context. The attempt by the United States to relativize the problem of torture has been interpreted by authoritarian regimes in Asia to mean that the old approach—the absolute prohibition of torture—is no longer respected by the international community. Thus, wherever there is armed conflict in Asia we find the period of legal detention extended, for the simple purpose of giving the authorities more time to torture people.

The theory of the ticking of the clock—that information must be obtained quickly from suspects to prevent terror plots—has been used to justify the widespread use of torture by intelligence agencies assisting military operations. Thus, the battle for the elimination of torture suffers from legal obstacles as well as a psychological climate that trivializes this principle.

Torture Is Still Common in Brazil

Brazzil Magazine

Brazzil Magazine *is a web-based, English-language magazine focusing on Brazilian politics and culture published in Los Angeles.*

In its latest periodic review of Brazil, international organization Human Rights Watch, whose mission is to protect human rights around the world, concludes that police violence in Brazil continues to be one of the country's most intractable human rights problems.

Faced with high levels of violent crime, the report says, especially in the country's urban centers, some police engage in abusive practices rather than pursuing sound policing policies. And the document continues:

> Prison conditions are abysmal. In rural regions, violence and land conflicts are ongoing, and human rights defenders suffer threats and attacks. And, while the Brazilian government has made efforts to redress human rights abuses, it has rarely held accountable those responsible for the violations.

The Lack of Public Security

Brazil continues to face major problems in the area of public security. The country's metropolitan areas, and especially their low-income neighborhoods (favelas), are plagued by widespread violence, perpetrated by criminal gangs, abusive police, and, in the case of Rio de Janeiro, militias reportedly linked to the police. Every year, roughly 50,000 people are murdered in Brazil.

In Rio [de Janeiro], criminal gangs launched a series of coordinated attacks against police officers, buses, and public buildings in December 2006, killing 11 people, including two officers. Reacting to the attacks, police killed seven people that they classified as suspects.

There have been credible reports of police and prison guards torturing people in their custody as a form of punishment, intimidation, and extortion.

Earlier in the year [2007], in São Paulo state, a criminal gang's coordinated attacks on police and public buildings led to clashes between police and gang members that resulted in the killing of more than 100 civilians and some 40 security agents in the state of São Paulo. A preliminary investigation by an independent committee found evidence that many of the killings documented during this period were extrajudicial executions.

According to official figures, police killed 694 people in the first six months of 2007 in Rio de Janeiro in situations described as "resistance followed by death," 33.5 percent more than in the same period last year. The number includes 44 people killed during a two-month police operation aimed at dismantling drug trafficking gangs in Complexo do Alemão, Rio de Janeiro's poorest neighborhood.

Violence reached a peak on June 27 [2007], when 19 people were killed during alleged confrontations with the police. According to residents and local nongovernmental organizations, many of the killings were summary executions. In October, at least 12 people were killed during a police incursion in Favela da Coréia, including a 4-year-old boy.

Police violence was also common in the state of São Paulo, where officers killed 201 people in the first half of 2007, according to official data. Fifteen officers were killed during the same period.

Torture by Police

Torture remains a serious problem in Brazil. The federal government's National Campaign against Torture reported receiving 1,336 complaints of torture between October 2001 and July 2003.

There have been credible reports of police and prison guards torturing people in their custody as a form of punishment, intimidation, and extortion. Police have also allegedly used torture as a means of obtaining information or coercing confessions from criminal suspects.

Abusive police officers are rarely sanctioned, and abuses are sometimes justified by authorities as an inevitable by-product of efforts to combat Brazil's very high crime rates.

Prison Conditions

The inhumane conditions, violence and overcrowding that have historically characterized Brazilian prisons remain one of the country's main human rights problems. According to the National Penitentiary Department, Brazilian prisons and jails held 419,551 inmates in June 2007, exceeding the system's capacity by approximately 200,000 inmates.

Violence continues to plague prisons around the country. In the first four months of 2007, 651 persons were killed while in detention, according to a parliamentary commission investigating problems in the country's prisons.

The commission was formed in August after 25 inmates burned to their death during a riot in a prison in Minas Gerais. In September, detainees in a prison in Manaus also staged a riot, killing two men. Riots also ended in deaths in overcrowded prisons in Recife and Abreu e Lima, in the state of Pernambuco.

At Urso Branco prison, in Rondônia, one prisoner died and at least seven were injured during an uprising in July. Since November 2000, at least 97 inmates have reportedly been killed at the facility. The Inter-American Court of Human Rights has ordered Brazil to adopt measures to guarantee the safety of inmates in Urso Branco on four occasions since 2002, but Brazil has failed to do so.

Overcrowding, rats, diseased pigeons, poor water quality and a lack of medication were among the problems reported by the São Paulo state public defender's office at Sant'Ana female penitentiary, in São Paulo. The office has repeatedly urged the closing of the facility, where five inmates died between December 2006 and June 2007.

Although children and adolescents are granted special protection under Brazilian and international law, they are subjected to serious abuses by the juvenile detention system. Young inmates are subject to violence by other youths or prison guards.

Human rights violations in Brazil are rarely prosecuted.

Forced Labor

The use of forced labor continues to be a problem in rural Brazil, despite government efforts to expose violations. Since 1995, when the federal government created mobile units to monitor labor conditions in rural areas, approximately 26,000 workers deemed to be working in conditions analogous to slavery were liberated.

From January to August 2007, Brazil's Ministry of Labor and Employment liberated over 3,400 workers, including a record of 1,064 people freed in a single operation on a farm in Pará in July.

Yet, according to the Pastoral Land Commission, a Catholic Church's group that defends the rights of rural workers, the number of reports that it receives of laborers working under slave-like conditions remains constant at 250 to 300 a year, involving between 6,000 and 8,000 workers, but the government investigates only half of these cases.

As of August 2007, no one had been punished for maintaining workers in slave-like conditions, according to the head of the public prosecutor's division responsible for combating slave labor.

Impunity

Human rights violations in Brazil are rarely prosecuted. In an effort to remedy this problem, the Brazilian government passed a constitutional amendment in 2004 that makes human rights crimes federal offenses.

It allows certain human rights violations to be transferred from the state to the federal justice system for investigation and trial. The transfer, however, can only happen if requested by the Federal Prosecutor General and accepted by the Superior Tribunal of Justice. To date, there have been no such transfers.

In a positive step, the trial for the 2005 murder of Dorothy Stang, an American missionary who fought for agrarian reform, resulted in the conviction and sentencing of three men in May 2007. Because two of them received sentences greater than 20 years of imprisonment, however, they had the right to new trials. One of them was already retried and convicted to 27 years.

Brazil has never prosecuted those responsible for atrocities committed in the period of military rule (1964–1985). An amnesty law passed in 1979 pardoned both government agents and members of armed political groups who had committed abuses.

The Brazilian federal government released in August 2007 a report on the results of an 11-year investigation by the national Commission on Political Deaths and Disappearances to determine the fate of government opponents who were killed or "disappeared" by state security forces between 1961 and 1988.

The commission was unable to clarify important aspects of these crimes, including the whereabouts of the majority of the "disappeared," because the Brazilian armed forces have never opened key archives from the military years.

In September [2007], the Superior Tribunal of Justice ordered the armed forces to open secret files and reveal what happened to the remains of Brazilians who died or disappeared when the government sent troops to fight the Araguaia guerrilla uprising in 1971.

Police in India Frequently Use Torture

Rama Lakshmi

Indian journalist Rama Lakshmi writes for the Washington Post Foreign Service.

Rajeev Sharma, a young electrician, was sleeping when police barged into his house ... [in 2004] and dragged him out of bed on suspicion of a burglary in the neighborhood, his family recalled.

When his young wife and brother protested, the police, who did not show them an arrest warrant, said they were taking Sharma to the police station for "routine questioning."

"Little did we know that we would lose him forever," said Sunil Sharma, Rajeev's brother, recounting how he died while in police custody. "Their routine questioning proved fatal," he added, sitting beside his brother's grieving widow.

[There is] frequent use of torture and deadly force at local police stations in India, a practice decried by human rights activists and the Indian Supreme Court.

Rajeev Sharma, 28, died at the police station within a day of his detention. Police said he committed suicide, but his family charges that he was beaten and killed.

Torture in India

The case highlights the frequent use of torture and deadly force at local police stations in India, a practice decried by human rights activists and the Indian Supreme Court. A little

Rama Lakshmi, "In India, Torture by Police Is Frequent and Often Deadly," *The Washington Post*, August 5, 2004. www.washingtonpost.com. Reproduced by permission of the author.

more than a decade after Parliament established the National Human Rights Commission to deal with such abuses, police torture continues unabated, according to human rights groups and the Indian Supreme Court. According to the latest available government data, there were 1,307 reported deaths in police and judicial custody in India in 2002.

"India has the highest number of cases of police torture and custodial deaths among the world's democracies and the weakest law against torture," said Ravi Nair, who heads the South Asia Human Rights Documentation Center. "The police often operate in a climate of impunity, where torture is seen as routine police behavior to extract confessions from small pickpockets to political suspects." He said that laws governing police functions were framed under British colonial rule in 1861 "as an oppressive force designed to keep the population under control."

Although the Indian government signed the international Convention Against Torture in 1997, it has not ratified the document.

Tortured to Death

Police records show that, two weeks before his detention, Rajeev Sharma made a electrician's service call at the home of a wealthy businessman. On that day, the man reported that $500 worth of gold jewelry and about $100 in cash were missing, police said.

After Sharma's detention, his brother called the police station and was told that Sharma had confessed to the theft, he said. The brother said he and other family members rushed to the station and were able to see Sharma briefly.

"His eyes were red, his mouth was bleeding and he could hardly walk. They had beaten him very badly. That was the last glimpse we had," said Sunil Sharma, 35. "By the evening, the police informed us that he had committed suicide in the lockup by hanging himself with a blanket. The suicide story is a coverup; my brother died of police torture."

The death in police custody sparked two days of rioting and protests in Meerut, about 45 miles from New Delhi, in the northern state of Uttar Pradesh. Angry residents surrounded and threw stones at the police station, burned police vehicles and blocked traffic.

Thousands participated in Sharma's funeral procession; protesters demanded an open inquest by a panel of physicians and the immediate arrests of those responsible.

Police conducted an autopsy in private, lawyers close to the case said. But authorities did issue arrest warrants for the man who said he had been robbed and for six police officers, an apparent reaction to the unusual popular outcry, family members and lawyers said. The merchant is in jail, alleged to have participated in beating Sharma, but the police officers apparently have fled, authorities said.

Some police officers justify the use of torture to extract confessions and instill fear.

The Government's Position

Although the Indian government signed the international Convention Against Torture in 1997, it has not ratified the document. Some members of Parliament have argued against ratification, saying they oppose international scrutiny and asserting that Indian laws have adequate provisions to prevent torture. Human rights advocates said Uttar Pradesh ranks highest among Indian states in the incidence of police torture and custodial deaths.

Some police officers justify the use of torture to extract confessions and instill fear.

Al Qaeda Terrorists Carried On Saddam Hussein's Gruesome Torture Techniques in Iraq

Entifadh Qanbar

Entifadh Qanbar is an Iraqi politician who served as spokesman of the Iraqi National Congress and as the deputy military attaché for Iraq in Washington, D.C.

Recently, the Iraqi military and the coalition forces have discovered torture houses run by Al Qaeda in Iraq.

The Atrocity Sites

To obtain an accurate picture of the level of atrocities committed by this band of thugs, it is first necessary to review what the American military rightly calls the "atrocity sites." I saw pictures of the bodies of victims found in these houses showing burned feet, open wounds, cut limbs, dislocated shoulders and joints which were the grisly results of hanging and beating and other horrific methods of torture.

I have researched and spoken with several American military officers concerning these torture houses. Here is a brief description of these houses which were discovered:

- Baquoba, June 2007: Discovery of the first torture house. Victims had drill holes in their bodies and deep gouges caused by blow torches; an Al Qaeda flag was in the torture house; many of the torture wounds were in the bottom of the feet of the victims. Torture equipment included: Drills, blow torches, chains hanging from the walls and ceiling, blood trails, saws, drills,

Entifadh Qanbar, "School of Torture," *New York Sun*, March 4, 2008. www.nysun.com. Reproduced by permission.

knives, weapons, masks, and handcuffs. An execution site outside of building where Iraqi victims were lined up and shot.

- Khan Bani Saad, August 2007: Discovery of rooms filled with torture tools and murdered Iraqi victims.

- Arab Jibour, near Dora, south of Baghdad, August 2007: Blood splattered on the walls. Piles of corpses found outside the house.

- Tarmiyya, September 2007: Nine prisoners were freed; many victims had been chained in place.

- Muqdadiyah, December 2007: Beds wired for electrical shock with electricity still on. Masks, whips, bloody knives, and chains hanging from ceiling on the site. Twenty-six bodies found buried on site: most had hands tied and were shot in the head. Locals said Al Qaeda was intimidating the area with threats of torture and execution.

After the liberation of Iraq in 2003, the world was finally able to obtain an unprecedented glimpse into the Baath torture chambers.

The Link Between Al Qaeda and the Baathists

I am an Iraqi who has suffered under Saddam's harsh dictatorship and who actively fought Saddam [Hussein] for many years before the liberation in 2003. In addition, I participated in the reconstruction efforts in the new Iraq after the liberation, and therefore have a unique perspective to offer in understanding the progression of events in modern day Iraq. I had my first taste of Saddam's brutality when I was imprisoned by Saddam's Military Security in 1987 along with my brother. In spite of my relatively short stay in a horrifying cell,

I witnessed torture and humiliation first hand in what seemed to be an underworld in which pain and degradation have no end.

For Iraqis, these torture chambers and "atrocity sites" are a confirmation of the links between the terror of the Baath regime [the government run by the now-deceased dictator Saddam Hussein] and that of Al Qaeda. In 1991, during the uprising in Iraqi Kurdistan, Iraqis and the outside world were able to see torture cells from the inside and bear witness to the gruesome acts performed within them for the first time.

After the liberation of Iraq in 2003, the world was finally able to obtain an unprecedented glimpse into the Baath torture chambers and the vast security apparatus which served to maintain order and cement Saddam's power over Iraq.

The old ways of the Baath regime have carried over into the present.

If you enter a torture house, you would think it is almost identical to a mechanical workshop: it contains drills, blow torches, hammers, and electrical wiring. For Saddam's agents, these houses of torture contain all the necessary hardware to extract information from the brains of detainees and very creative ways to punish and extract victims. Thus torture cells established by Saddam's agents were a horrific instrument of spreading terror and maintaining the iron grip of the regime over the country.

The old ways of the Baath regime have carried over into the present. Information on one of the Al Qaeda computers confiscated by the American military contains a manual illustrated with what almost appear to be children's school drawings on how to use drills, gouge out eyes, use blow torches to burn the bottom of victim's feet, suspend people in chains, cut limbs, and enact other gruesome ways of torture.

The Awakening

Initially, torture houses were an effective way to threaten Iraqis locally and to consolidate the power of Al Qaeda in the zones of its operation. These houses served as a painful reminder of the 35 years of the brutality and suppression of the old Baath regime. But Iraqis are not willing to go back to the old days of Saddam's regime. These practices by Al Qaeda and other methods of oppression, totalitarianism, and humiliation towards the population resulted in what we see today as the "awakening."

It began with members of the Sunni population who thought that their future would be better with the insurgents like Al Qaeda—the same people who invited Al Qaeda into their areas, who provided help to foreign fighters coming to areas such [as] Al Qaem, Fallujah. These people were the first to discover the misery and horror the insurgents were truly offering to them behind an attractive façade, and began to take steps to retaliate and unite against groups like Al Qaeda in Iraq. I appreciate their honesty in calling the movement an "awakening" because it shows a level of responsibility and acknowledgment for past errors.

Baathists and Saddam's former security elements taught Al Qaeda members certain methods of fighting and torture.

In places other than Iraq that have been struggling with an Al Qaeda presence for years, such as Afghanistan, there is no record of the discovery of torture houses. Despite the many years of brutal fighting against Muslim extremists and Al Qaeda in Algeria, to date no discovery of torture houses has been made in that country either.

Reports from battle grounds in Iraq tell of strong resistance and deadly fighting by Al Qaeda operatives around these houses. The commonplace assumption that Al Qaeda will not work with Saddam's Baathist elements because the first are religious and the latter are purely secular is simply not true. Thus the marriage of convenience between these two groups is to obtain information from victims and kill a common enemy—America—and any perceived local supporters. This aim achieves goals that are in the interests of each party; terrorists do not discriminate to achieve their goals and principles come second to power.

A New Breed of Al Qaeda

What has made Al Qaeda in Iraq so different from Al Qaeda in the rest of the world? The answer is simple. Baathists and Saddam's former security elements taught Al Qaeda members certain methods of fighting and torture.

I am not underestimating Al Qaeda operatives in their capabilities to fight and practice extreme brutality. However, in Iraq, Al Qaeda operatives found that Saddam's elements were ready to teach them new techniques of fighting and provide them with necessary logistical and operational support. This led to a sharpening of the capabilities of Al Qaeda in Iraq. The combination of young Arab fanatics with the techniques and the experience of the Baath elements has resulted in the emergence of a new breed of Al Qaeda.

Over the past 12 years, I have observed many good days and numerous setbacks in Iraq, yet I have never lost hope in a positive outcome for the future of my country. We are witnessing the last phase and the end of terrorism in Iraq on a large scale.

The foreign fighters who were able to stay alive are migrating back to their own countries of origin and elsewhere in the world. Intelligence information shows these foreign fighters, although small in number in Iraq, are lethal and ruthless. Many of these young fighters came to Iraq and are now leaving well-trained in all types of fighting, having acquired methods and techniques from Saddam's former Republican Guard, Intelligence, and Security members.

These fighters have learned valuable techniques in Iraq, such as how to perfect the art of making improvised explosive devices, in addition to gaining expertise in constructing car bombs and organizing combat leadership. These highly-trained fighters are leaving Iraq as the war on terror is nearing its end in my country.

They are certain to go to back to their countries and other fields of battle at the peak of their energy armed with extensive first-hand knowledge. I expect that they will become leaders of terror organizations and they will take terrorism in their countries and elsewhere to a higher and more sophisticated level. Much of the world has overlooked what has happened in Iraq and has regarded the war on terror as a failure. Now things are changing, and those who have overlooked the development of such events in Iraq must subsequently alter their perceptions if they are to combat the influx of these fighters and prevent the outbreak of violence beyond Iraq's borders.

CHAPTER 2

Is Torture Morally Wrong?

Chapter Overview

Sherry F. Colb

Sherry F. Colb was on staff at Columbia Law School when the following viewpoint was written, and is now a law professor at Cornell Law School in Ithaca, New York.

Whether torture is ever justifiable is, to put it mildly, controversial. In the age of global terrorism, one can easily imagine scenarios in which torture could mean the difference between life and death for innocent civilians. Numerous scholars have weighed in on this issue, and those who disagree with one another often have difficulty remaining civil in their discourse.

Nonetheless, a common assumption underlies virtually everything that moral theorists say on the subject—the assumption that "torture is different." Nearly everyone assumes that unlike other things that people do to one another (including killing each other in ways that knowingly—though not deliberately—cause the same sorts of excruciating pain as torture does), torture demands a different form of analysis. While there are pacifists, who oppose all violence, many absolute opponents of torture—such as Amnesty International—are not pacifists. Yet there seems to be a broad consensus that torture is different and that distinct rules ought to apply....

One camp believes that torture is always and necessarily wrong.

The Moral Terrain

When we debate the legitimacy of torture, the scope of argument is relatively narrow. Moral theorists tend to agree that nearly all instances of torture known to humankind are un-

Sherry F. Colb, "Why Is Torture 'Different' and How 'Different' Is It?" *Cardozo Law Review*, vol. 30, 2009. http://papers.ssrn.com. Reproduced by permission.

justifiable. Such instances include the conduct of the Spanish and Portuguese Inquisitions [15th–19th centuries], the Nazis during the second World War [1939–45], the French in Algeria [1954–62], official acts during Argentina's dirty war [1976–83], and the more recent, photographically documented, behavior of American soldiers at Abu Ghraib [a U.S. detention facility in Iraq], along with what is generally thought to be routine conduct in regimes such as Egypt, Jordan, Syria, and Morocco, to which the U.S. has been accused of sending terrorist suspects in a practice known as "extraordinary rendition."

Some of the strongest defenders of justifiable torture agree with its absolute opponents that most examples of torture—motivated by hatred, sadism, the desire for incriminating evidence, and a search for preventative information on a flimsy foundation—are indefensible. Even an unapologetic proponent of its permissibility under limited circumstances, describes torture as "monstrous."

In the other camp ... people share the view that torture might be justifiable on rare occasions.

Notwithstanding such wide consensus, the disagreements—though narrow—generate heated and angry debate. Roughly organized, one camp believes that torture is always and necessarily wrong. The duty to refrain from torture is absolute, on this approach, and may not bend, no matter how strong ... the interests on the other side. This is also the position of existing law, including the U.N. Convention Against Torture and Other Cruel, Inhuman, and Degrading Treatment or Punishment, to which the United States is a signatory. It is, as well, the view of such NGOs [non-governmental organizations] as Human Rights Watch and Amnesty International. Even when faced with tragic hypothetical examples, their response is unconditional: no torture, ever.

In the other camp (which is itself composed of differing perspectives), people share the view that torture might be justifiable on rare occasions. Members of this camp are willing to entertain, as a thought experiment, the so-called "ticking bomb" scenario—a hypothetical case in which authorities have in custody a terrorist who has set a bomb that will imminently explode and kill many people unless the captors torture the terrorist into revealing where the bomb is, thereby saving the lives that would otherwise have been lost. Members of the second camp find themselves unwilling to say no to torture under the hypothesized circumstances. In their view, faced with the prospect of the deaths of thousands of innocent lives, we may—and, by some accounts, must—torture the terrorist to save the civilians.

Though they share this impulse about the ticking bomb case, members of the second camp divide on the question of how that impulse should affect the legal status of torture. To prevent *unjustified* torture, some theorists who accept that torture is justified in the ticking bomb case nonetheless say that the law must categorically ban it. Furthermore, once a justifiable act of torture occurs, those who support a ban divide on what the consequences for the torturer ought to be. On one view, the torturer must accept his punishment, as all brave practitioners of civil disobedience do as the price for justifiably violating the law under extreme circumstances. A competing approach supports a torturer's access to a common law criminal defense such as necessity or self-defense. And of those who find the ticking bomb scenario a compelling basis for torture, some would allow the law to reflect the justification directly. They might, for example, support a pre-ordained authorization or immunity from prosecution, such as the torture warrants advocated by [Harvard Law Professor] Alan Dershowitz. Still others not only view torture as justified in a variety of circumstances but understand the prohibitions against torture to apply very narrowly or not at all in the interrogational context. The last of these approaches might fairly be characterized as demonstrating far less hostility to torture than all of the others do. . . .

Intriguingly, Alan Dershowitz refuses to say unequivocally that there are cases in which torture would be justified, though he claims that as a normative matter, he would like to see torture minimized or eliminated. He is therefore the only major theorist who might actually fall into the first camp (of those who believe that torture is always wrong, no matter what the circumstances might be), while at the same time proposing a legal approach that explicitly tolerates some torture and does so both officially and *ex ante* (thus insulating the torturer from later prosecution). Perhaps it is the inherent tension between suggesting that something is categorically wrong, on the one hand, and proposing that it should nonetheless be officially sanctioned, on the other, that accounts for the strongly negative reception that Dershowitz's ideas have received in both the scholarly and general literature. It makes him an easy target for those, like William Shulz [executive director of Amnesty International USA], who ask rhetorically whether Dershowitz would favor warrants authorizing official perjury, police brutality, and prison rape as well. . . .

Because one's own philosophical views invariably color one's account of all philosophical positions, fairness requires me to disclose my own approach: I would count myself among the moral hybrids. I care deeply about the consequences of people's actions, but I also consider some actions, under some circumstances, sufficiently wrong to require restraint even when the wrongful means would result in a net gain.

Torture Is Morally Reprehensible

Kim Petersen

Kim Petersen is co-editor of Dissident Voice, *a Web site that provides news and commentary on politics and culture.*

Treat others as you wish to be treated yourself. It is basic common sense for most people. We should not expect to be treated any differently or better than how we ourselves treat others. This . . . is elementary morality.

The results from an AP-Ipsos [a research and polling group] poll conducted between 15 November and 28 November [2005] gives pause to people's grasp of elementary morality. The poll reveals that in some countries there is substantial support for the notion that torture of suspected terrorists can be justifiable. Important to note is that the poll is not talking about convicted terrorists but rather "suspected terrorists." This is disturbing because the presumption of innocence has been dismissed. German citizen Khaled al-Masri's desperate plight speaks to this. Masri was abducted by the CIA [Central Intelligence Agency], transferred to another country, tortured and subsequently released after the "mistake" became apparent.

The poll raises many questions. For example, who is defining terrorism? Can the right to torture suspected terrorists be justified when the alleged terrorists are resisting an illegal invasion and occupation . . . ?

Poll Results

Approximately 1,000 adults were interviewed in each of the nine countries traditionally considered strong allies of the United States. The margin of error for each poll was plus or

Kim Petersen, "Elementary Morality and Torture," *Dissident Voice,* December 7, 2005. www.dissidentvoice.org. Reproduced by permission of the author.

minus 3.1 percentage points. Much of the support for justifiable torture . . . is limited to "rare instances." Has anyone ever heard of the slippery slope argument?

The poll results indicate that support for justifiable torture is highest in southern Korea and the United States. There is also strong support in the United Kingdom and France with borderline results in Germany, Canada, and Mexico. Italians and Spaniards are opposed.

Whether torture is illegal or not is a side argument. Torture is morally reprehensible.

When respondents were asked about how they felt about the US interrogating suspected terrorists in their country, the results were strongly in opposition in every country except the US, where 63 percent indicated support.

U.S. Torture

Disregarding mendacious denials from high-ranking US officials, it is no secret that the United States is running a worldwide system of detention centers where torture is used on prisoners. In carrying out its so-called War on Terrorism . . . the US government has contorted international laws and conventions to its own twisted aims. The US government has cowardly eluded the international protections afforded prisoners of war through the introduction of its own designation of "enemy combatants"—a designation not provided for in international law. The US is sending a dangerous signal: it is very easy to slip from the constraints of international law; all that is required is to coin new terminology.

Whether torture is illegal or not is a side argument. Torture is morally reprehensible. It debases humanity to its most atavistic level. If the US government cared for the safety of its captured forces . . . then it would oppose torture and enforce an international prohibition against it. The US attempts to shield its troops from their war crimes in Iraq through questionable occupation legislation and failure to accede to the authority of the International Criminal Court ... but ... US troops are left vulnerable on the ground. The US fighters themselves should be refusing torture with all their force. Their very use of torture exposes themselves and fellow fighters ... that fall into "enemy" hands to a similar treatment. Obviously for many US troops, the appeal to morality is in vain but this does not involve morality. It is just an appeal to the self-preservation instinct.

Republican US Senator John McCain ... was himself a victim of torture in Vietnam. He is a leading proponent to ban the use of torture as well as "cruel and inhumane treatment." The anti-torture legislation was heavily approved in the Senate [in 2005] but the war president George [W.] Bush has indicated that he will veto the measure. [Bush signed the bill in December 2005 but reserved the right to bypass the torture ban under his powers as commander-in-chief.]

The questions used in the AP-Ipsos poll are leading. The poll might have asked: "How do you feel about the use of torture against people who might be innocent to obtain information about terrorist activities of which they might know nothing about?" This might have led to completely different results. Nonetheless, the use of torture is but one further instance of the regressive slope trod by the Bush government in its never-ending crusades. The sadness is that so many people in the western world would slide down this slope. It bodes ill for humanity.

Torture Is Always Morally Wrong

David P. Gushee

David P. Gushee is an author and a professor of moral philosophy at Union University in Jackson, Tennessee.

The word "torture," tellingly, comes from the Latin *torquere*, to twist. Stine Amris and Julio G. Arenas, who have done extensive studies on the effects of torture, define it as "the infliction of severe pain (whether physical or psychological) by a perpetrator who acts purposefully and on behalf of the state.". . .

The Torture Debate

The debate in our nation today concerns what measures can legitimately be taken to extract information from prisoners held by us in the "war on terror" and the wars in Afghanistan and Iraq. As such, it is a debate about the proper use of government power in a liberal democracy. Can that power ever rightly extend to the use of any form of torture?

Few people disagree that a liberal democracy has the right and responsibility to take prisoners and interrogate them during a war or police action. This is part of the government's biblical mandate in Romans 13:1-7, a mandate to deter violations of peace and justice. Most would even agree that interrogators should have some flexibility in applying pressure to encourage prisoners to reveal information that could save lives. The question is whether torture can be included among the forms of pressure that can legitimately be employed.

As to the exact kinds of acts that constitute torture, there is no single definition, but this does not mean that the term is

David P. Gushee, "5 Reasons Torture Is Always Wrong; and Why There Should Be No Exceptions," *Christianity Today*, vol. 50, no. 2, February 1, 2006. www.christianitytoday.com. Reproduced by permission of the author.

infinitely elastic. . . . International agreements have repeatedly sought to define torture as they have denounced it. The 1948 Universal Declaration of Human Rights states that "no one shall be subjected to torture or to cruel, inhuman, or degrading treatment." Article 17 of the Third Geneva Convention (1949) asserts that "no physical or mental torture, nor any other form of coercion, may be inflicted on prisoners of war," but, instead, "persons taking no active part in the hostilities . . . shall in all circumstances be treated humanely." The 1985 U.N. Convention Against Torture defines it as "any act by which severe pain or suffering, whether physical or mental, is intentionally inflicted on a person." The United States is a signatory to all of these international declarations and has historically incorporated their principles into military doctrine. For example, the 1992 U.S. Army Field Manual tells soldiers that "[Geneva] and U.S. policy expressly prohibit acts of violence or intimidation, including physical or mental torture, threats [or] insults, . . . as a means of or aid to interrogation."

The Bush administration has . . . attempted to carve out room for acts that brush up against the boundary line separating aggressive interrogation from torture.

The kinds of acts most often classified as torture make for a dreary catalog of pain. They include physical torture, beatings, use of electric shock, employment of mind-altering drugs, sexual assault, and various other inventive ways of harming the bodies and minds of other human beings.

Torture Lite

When the current U.S. President [George W. Bush] repeatedly says that "we do not torture," perhaps these kinds of acts are what he has in mind. But since [the terrorist attacks of] September 11, 2001, the Bush administration has, in the name of national security, attempted to carve out room for acts that brush up against the boundary line separating aggressive interrogation from torture, without (they believe) crossing over it. Called "enhanced interrogation techniques," "professional interrogation," "moderate physical pressure," or even . . . "torture lite," these have included a variety of measures, some approved as policy by our government and others not publicly acknowledged or approved. But both independent and government investigators have discovered that such techniques have been used in U.S. detention facilities.

Among the sometimes approved measures have been prolonged standing, removal of detainees' clothing, sensory deprivation, hooding (often with smelly hoods), prolonged interrogations, use of dogs, forced shaving of beards, grabbing, poking, pushing, sleep manipulation and deprivation, and waterboarding (which refers to a variety of techniques designed to make a victim feel as if he were drowning).

Among the unapproved but practiced measures have been punching, slapping, and kicking detainees, religious and sexual humiliation, prolonged shackling, exposure to severe heat or cold, food or toilet deprivation, mock or threatened executions, and letting dogs threaten or in some cases bite and severely injure detainees.

The abuses appear to have been particularly prevalent in CIA [Central Intelligence Agency] interrogations, among private U.S. contractors serving the military, and among the underprepared and poorly trained military police at places like Abu Ghraib [a U.S. prison] in Iraq. There are also profound worries and disturbing allegations about what is going on with "high-value" detainees in CIA interrogations at undisclosed locations.

Though [Secretary of State] Condoleezza Rice has said that prisoners in U.S. custody anywhere in the world should be afforded the same protections as if they were on U.S. soil, some still wonder about the significance of these assurances—and especially about what is happening to prisoners "rendered" by our government to other countries (many known to practice torture).

Furthermore, while all "cruel, inhuman, or degrading" treatment of detainees has been officially rejected by the administration ... it is not clear who defines when treatment crosses that line. It also remains unclear how much latitude those on the front lines of interrogation have, and if and how they would be held accountable if they were to cross the line. In other words, there remain a number of loopholes for torture to be practiced in the war on terror.

Yet the prohibition on torture in international law admits no exceptions. The U.N. Convention Against Torture puts it this way: "No exceptional circumstances whatsoever, whether a state of war or a threat of war, internal political instability or any other public emergency, may be invoked as a justification for torture."

The U.S. ratified this convention in 1994, before September 11, before we launched our war on terror. Despite the passage of the McCain Amendment against torture [in 2005], many Americans and some leading administration officials continue to believe that acts tantamount to torture are morally permissible in the exceptional case posed by Islamist terrorism. As State Department official Cofer Black famously put it: "All I want to say is that there was before 9/11 and after 9/11. After 9/11, the gloves came off."

Because they are human, people have rights to many things, including the right not to be tortured.

Christian Views on Torture

How should a Christian think about all this?

Let me begin by granting that the terrorist attacks of September 11 were one of the most heinous acts ever visited upon this nation, a clear violation of the laws of war and any kind of civilized moral code. Since then, terrorist acts around the world remind us that our nation, along with many others, faces a threat from enemies who do not adhere to the kinds of moral scruples we are considering ... [here].

So I do not write to demonize those who believe that protecting our nation's security requires the use of interrogation techniques that could be classified as borderline torture. Nor do I want to get into a technical and detailed argument about particular interrogation techniques to determine if they are torture. What I want to focus on is the idea that, given the war on terror, the gloves should be taken off. Simply put, should our government have the option—even if used only rarely and in extreme circumstances—of torturing prisoners?

I believe Christians should say no, on the following five grounds.

1. *Torture violates the dignity of the human being.* Every inch of the human body and every aspect of the human spirit comes from God and bears witness to his handiwork. We are made in the image of God. Human dignity, value, and worth come as a permanent and ineradicable endowment of the Creator to every person.

Christians, at least, should be trained to see in every person the imprint of God's grandeur. This should create in us a sense of reverence. Here, we say—and we say it even of detainees in the war on terror—is a human being sacred in God's sight, made in God's image, someone for whom Christ died. No one is ever "subhuman" or "human debris," as Rush Limbaugh has described some of our adversaries in Iraq.

Those who have been tortured are victims of injustice.

Because they are human, people have rights to many things, including the right not to be tortured. Christians sometimes question the legitimacy of "rights talk," correctly so. Just because someone claims a right does not mean that it really is a right. But among the most widely recognized rights in both legal and moral theory is the right to bodily integrity; that is, the right not to have intentional physical and psychological harm inflicted upon oneself by others. The ban on torture is one expression of this right.

Is this right absolute? Using Catholic moral reasoning, Robert G. Kennedy, professor of Catholic studies at the University of St. Thomas in St. Paul, Minnesota, has argued that even the most widely recognized human rights, such as the right to life or the right not to be tortured, can theoretically be qualified by other rights and by the requirements of justice. Kennedy argues that "defensive interrogatory torture" (and only this kind of torture) may be morally legitimate under carefully qualified conditions. Yet he goes on to argue that "it is quite likely that most instances in which interrogatory torture is employed would not conform to these principles and so would be immoral."

Whether we open the door to torture just a crack, as Kennedy suggests, or keep it firmly shut as an absolute ban, as I advocate, the principle of human dignity and correlated rights remains a transcendently important reason to resist the turn toward torture.

Authorizing even the "lightest" forms of torture risks abuse.

---

2. *Torture mistreats the vulnerable and violates the demands of justice.* In the Scriptures, God's understanding of justice tilts toward the vulnerable. "Do not mistreat an alien or oppress him, for you were aliens in Egypt. Do not take advantage of a widow or an orphan. If you do and they cry out to me, I will certainly hear their cry." Primary forms of injustice include violent abuse and domination of the powerless.

One reason our legal system has so many layers of protection for the accused and imprisoned is their powerlessness. This is important in any legal system that has the power to deprive people of their liberty and even their lives. The 83,000 people who have been detained by our government and military . . . [since the war on terror began in September 2001] are, as prisoners, vulnerable to injustice. Those who have been tortured are victims of injustice.

3. *Authorizing torture trusts government too much.* Human beings are sinful through and through. We are not to be trusted, and we are especially dangerous when in possession of unchecked power. This applies to all of us.

So it is likely that authorizing even the "lightest" forms of torture risks abuse. As [Catholic priest and writer] Richard John Neuhaus has put it, "We dare not trust ourselves to torture." Or as Gary Haugen [president of International Justice Mission, an international human rights agency] recently wrote, "Because the power of the state over detainees is exercised by fallen human beings, that power must be limited by clear boundaries, and individuals exercising such power must be transparently accountable."

Given human sinfulness, not only must people be told not to torture, we must also strengthen the structures of due process, accountability, and transparency that buttress those standards and make them less likely to be violated. This is what is so dangerous about the discovery of secret CIA prisons in Europe and "ghost detainees" who are located no one knows where. As Manfred Nowak, U.N. special rapporteur on torture, said at the time the CIA's secret prisons were revealed, "Every secret place of detention is a higher risk for ill treatment; that's the danger of secrecy." It is not enough for U.S. government officials to say they can be trusted to act "in keeping with our values"—not without due process, accountability, and transparency. No government is so virtuous as to overcome the laws of human nature, or to be beyond the need for democratic checks and balances.

Much ink has been spilled over how to handle the rare ticking-bomb cases, in which a prisoner has information that could save thousands of lives if only he can be made to talk by a certain deadline. Perhaps the most widely discussed proposal has been [Harvard Law School professor and civil liberties lawyer] Alan Dershowitz's suggestion that we permit torture only through a "torture warrant" signed by a judge or a very high government official, such as the President himself, who would therefore bear full legal, political, and moral responsibility.

> *Loosening longstanding restrictions on physical and mental cruelty risks the dehumanization not just of the tortured, but also of the torturers.*

This would be better than what we are doing now. But I think any potential resort to torture in rare, ticking-bomb cases would be better handled within the context of an outright ban. The grand moral tradition of civil disobedience, for example, specifies that there are instances in which obedience to laws must be overridden by loyalty to a higher moral obligation. These are usually unjust laws, but not always. [German theologian and Lutheran pastor] Dietrich Bonhoeffer participated in an assassination plot against Hitler, for instance, but he did not argue for rewriting moral prohibitions against political assassinations. He was prepared to let God and history be his judge. If a one-in-a-million instance were to emerge, in which a responsible official believed that a ban on torture must be overridden as a matter of emergency response, let him do so knowing that he would have to answer for his action before God, law, and neighbor. This is a long way from an official authorization for torture.

4. *Torture dehumanizes the torturer.* Mark Bowden, a military scholar and author of *Black Hawk Down*, believes that sometimes torture is the right choice. Even so, he worries, "How does one allow it, yet still control it? Sadism is deeply rooted in the human psyche. Every army has its share of soldiers who delight in kicking and beating bound captives. Men

in authority tend to abuse it—not all men, but many. As a mass, they should be assumed to lean toward abuse."

Loosening longstanding restrictions on physical and mental cruelty risks the dehumanization not just of the tortured, but also of the torturers. What may be intended as carefully calibrated interrogation techniques could easily tempt implementers toward sadism—the infliction of pain for the sheer fun of it, especially in the heat of military conflict, in a climate of fear and loathing of the enemy, and in the context of an endless war on terror. How many of us could be trusted to draw the line consistently between the permitted "grabbing, poking, and pushing" and the banned "punching, slapping, and kicking"? How much self-control can we reasonably expect people to exercise? Once the line has been crossed to torture, as [Canadian author, academic, and politician] Michael Ignatieff claims, it "inflicts irremediable harm on both the torturer and the prisoner."

Torture erodes the character of the nation that tortures.

[Nineteenth-century abolitionist leader] Frederick Douglass commented famously on how holding a slave slowly ruined the character of the woman who owned him. [Civil rights leader] Martin Luther King Jr. frequently said that the greatest victims of segregation were the white people whose souls were deformed by their own hatred. And [Russian writer and Nobel laureate] Alexander Solzhenitsyn, reflecting on the Soviet gulag, said, "Our torturers have been punished most horribly of all: They are turning into swine; they are departing downward from humanity."

5. *Torture erodes the character of the nation that tortures.* A nation is a collective moral entity with a character, an identity that carries across time. Causes come and go, threats come and go, but the enduring question for any social entity is who

we are as a people. This is true of a family, a church, a school, a civic club, or a town. It is certainly true of a nation.

Sen. John McCain, who has led the Republican charge against torture, recently said, "This isn't about who they are. This is about who we are. These are the values that distinguish us from our enemies."

In a November [2005] *Newsweek* article, he put it this way: "What I . . . mourn is what we lose when . . . we allow, confuse, or encourage our soldiers to forget that best sense of ourselves, that which is our greatest strength—that we are different and better than our enemies, that we fight for an idea, not a tribe, not a land, not a king . . . but for an idea that all men are created equal and endowed by their Creator with inalienable rights."

No Exceptions

Long ago, German philosopher Immanuel Kant wrote about the perennial human tendency to find exceptions to moral rules when the rules bind a bit too tightly on us: "Hence there arises a natural . . . disposition to argue against these strict laws of duty and to question their validity, or at least their purity and strictness, and, if possible, to make them more accordant with our wishes and inclinations, that is to say, to corrupt them at their very source, and to entirely destroy their worth."

I believe this is the best explanation for what is happening with the issue of torture in our nation. We are tempted to follow the logic of a July 11, 2005 *Time* magazine cover story that said, "In the war on terrorism, the personal dignity of a fanatic trained for mass murder may be an inevitable casualty."

Yet we are queasy enough about this "inevitable casualty" that we do not want to call torture what it is. We do not want to expose our policies, our prisons, or our prisoners to public view. We deny that we are torturing, or we deny that our prisoners are really prisoners. When pushed against the wall, we remind one another how evil the enemy is. We give every evidence of the kind of self-deception that is characteristic of a descent into sin.

It is past time for evangelical Christians to remind our government and our society of perennial moral values, which also happen to be international and domestic laws. As Christians, we care about moral values, and we vote on the basis of such values. We care deeply about human-rights violations around the world. Now it is time to raise our voice and say an unequivocal no to torture, a practice that has no place in our society and violates our most cherished moral convictions.

People Around the World Agree That Torture Is Immoral

Mirela Xanthaki

Mirela Xanthaki is a reporter for Inter Press Service, *a global provider of independent news and editorial content.*

A new poll on the official use of torture shows that people worldwide oppose it, but more than one-third also say an exception should be made if it can extract information from "terrorists" to "save innocent lives."

While 35 percent agreed with this exception, just nine percent favoured allowing governments to use torture in general.

Poll Results

The poll results were issued by the University of Maryland's Programme on International Policy Attitudes (PIPA), in collaboration with a worldwide network of research centres, in advance of the International Day in Support of Victims of Torture on Jun. 26 [2008]. The poll was conducted in 19 nations, with 19,000 people responding to questions regarding the acceptance of the use of torture, as well as on the continuing prevalence of torture worldwide.

The nations surveyed were China, India, the United States, Indonesia, Nigeria, Russia, Mexico, Britain, France, Poland, Spain, Azerbaijan, Ukraine, Egypt, the Palestinian territories, Iran, Turkey, Thailand, and South Korea, together representing 60 percent of the world population.

Respondents were presented with an argument in favour of allowing the torture of potential terrorists who threaten civilians: "Terrorists pose such an extreme threat that govern-

Mirela Xanthaki, "Rights: Torture Widely Viewed as 'Immoral,'" *Inter Press Service*, 2008. www.ipsnews.net. Reproduced by permission.

ments should now be allowed to use some degree of torture if it may gain information that would save innocent lives."

In 14 nations, a majority or plurality rejected this argument in favour of the unequivocal view: "Clear rules against torture should be maintained because any use of torture is immoral and will weaken international human rights standards against torture."

In all nations polled, the number saying that the government should generally be able to use torture is less than one in five.

Those who favoured an exception for terrorists were also asked whether governments should generally be allowed to use torture. On average across all nations polled, just 9 percent said there should be no rules against torture.

China and Turkey had the largest percentages (18 percent in both) in favour of the idea that governments should generally be allowed to torture, while France and Britain (4 percent in both) had the lowest.

Out of the 19 nations included in the poll, 14 had a majority of people favour an unequivocal rule against torture, even in the case of terrorists who have information that could save innocent lives. On average across all nations polled, 57 percent opt for unequivocal rules against torture. The highest support for that was noted in Spain (82 percent), Britain (82 percent) and France (82 percent), followed by Mexico (73 percent), China (66 percent), the Palestinian territories (66 percent), Poland (62 percent), Indonesia (61 percent), and the Ukraine (59 percent).

Four nations lean toward favouring an exception in the case of terrorists—India (59 percent), Nigeria (54 percent), Turkey (51 percent), and a plurality in Thailand (44 percent).

However, large majorities in all 19 nations favour a general prohibition against torture. In all nations polled, the number saying that the government should generally be able to use torture is less than one in five.

In Azerbaijan (54 percent), Egypt (54 percent), the United States (53 percent), Russia (49 percent), and Iran (43 percent) a majority or plurality supported the ban on all torture.

The State of the World Report 2007 issued by Amnesty International highlights a number of governments believed to use torture. "The idea that torture by governments is basically wrong is widely shared in all corners of the world. Even the scenario one hears of terrorists holding information that could save innocent lives is rejected as a justification for torture in most countries," said Steven Kull, director of WorldPublicOpinion.org.

"Further," Kull adds, "since such a scenario is exceedingly rare, this poll suggests that virtually all torture used by governments is at odds with the will of the people."

As Yvonne Terlingen, Amnesty International's U.N. [United Nations] representative, noted at a press conference [in 2008] . . . "Only last week, the Human Rights council adopted a consensus resolution in Geneva which reaffirms the absolute prohibition of torture."

No circumstances can justify torture and no country openly agrees on torture, she said.

Shifts in Opinion

A 2006 poll conducted by PIPA found similar results, although there have been some dramatic shifts in specific countries. While in 2006, only India had a modest plurality favouring the exception of terrorists, Nigeria, Turkey and Thailand with a plurality now agree with that sentiment.

A substantial increase in support for using torture in the interrogation of terrorists was also seen in Egypt (from 25 percent to 46 percent) and the U.S. (from 36 percent to 44 percent).

At the same time, there has been an increase among those favouring a complete ban on torture in countries like Mexico, Spain, China, Indonesia, Britain and Russia.

The WorldPublicOpinion.org poll is part of a larger study on human rights issues being completed in conjunction with the 60th anniversary of the Universal Declaration of Human Rights. The study included other polls on topics like racial discrimination, women's rights, freedom of the press, democracy and governance.

Although there is very little confidence that governments are actually respecting the will of the people and there is a widely held belief that powerful interests are trumping the will of people, Craig Mokhiber from the Office of the High Commissioner for Human Rights talked about the "enormous strategic value of this survey."

"It allows us to see where we are going wrong, where additional attention needs to be paid in terms of governmental accountability and emerging threats," he said.

Torture Can Be a Moral Means of Saving Lives

Mirko Bagaric

Mirko Bagaric is professor of law and head of the Deakin Law School in Australia. The following viewpoint is a summary of a paper co-written with Julie Clarke, published by the University of San Francisco Law Review.

Recent events stemming from the "war on terrorism" have highlighted the prevalence of torture. This is despite the fact that torture is almost universally deplored. The formal prohibition against torture is absolute—there are no exceptions to it.

Torture Sometimes Justified

The belief that torture is always wrong is, however, misguided and symptomatic of the alarmist and reflexive responses typically emanating from social commentators. It is this type of absolutist and short-sighted rhetoric that lies at the core of many distorted moral judgements that we as a community continue to make, resulting in an enormous amount of injustice and suffering in our society and far beyond our borders.

Torture is permissible where the evidence suggests that this is the only means, due to the immediacy of the situation, to save the life of an innocent person. The reason that torture in such a case is defensible and necessary is because the justification manifests from the closest thing we have to an inviolable right: the right to self-defence, which of course extends to the defence of another. Given the choice between inflicting a relatively small level of harm on a wrongdoer and saving an innocent person, it is verging on moral indecency to prefer the interests of the wrongdoer.

The Hostage-Taking Scenario

The analogy with self-defence is sharpened by considering the hostage-taking scenario, where a wrongdoer takes a hostage and points a gun to the hostage's head, threatening to kill the hostage unless a certain (unreasonable) demand is met. In such a case it is not only permissible, but desirable for police to shoot (and kill) the wrongdoer if they get a "clear shot." This is especially true if it's known that the wrongdoer has a history of serious violence, and hence is more likely to carry out the threat.

There is no logical or moral difference between this scenario and one where there is overwhelming evidence that a wrongdoer has kidnapped an innocent person and informs police that the victim will be killed by a co-offender if certain demands are not met.

In the hostage scenario, it is universally accepted that it is permissible to violate the right to life of the aggressor to save an innocent person. How can it be wrong to violate an even less important right (the right to physical integrity) by torturing the aggressor in order to save a life in the second scenario?

Torture in order to save an innocent person is the only situation where it is clearly justifiable. This means that the recent high-profile incidents of torture, apparently undertaken as punitive measures or in a bid to acquire information where there was no evidence of an immediate risk to the life of an innocent person, were reprehensible.

Arguments Against Torture

There are three main counter-arguments to even the above limited approval of torture. The first is the slippery slope argument: if you start allowing torture in a limited context, the situations in which it will be used will increase.

This argument is not sound in the context of torture. First, the floodgates are already open—torture is used widely, despite the absolute legal prohibition against it. Amnesty International has recently reported that it had received, during 2003, reports of torture and ill-treatment from 132 countries, including the United States, Japan and France. It is, in fact, arguable that it is the existence of an unrealistic absolute ban that has driven torture beneath the radar of accountability, and that legalisation in very rare circumstances would in fact reduce instances of it.

The second main argument is that torture will dehumanise society. This is no more true in relation to torture than it is with self-defence, and in fact the contrary is true. A society that elects to favour the interests of wrongdoers over those of the innocent, when a choice must be made between the two, is in need of serious ethical rewiring.

A third counter-argument is that we can never be totally sure that torturing a person will in fact result in us saving an innocent life. This, however, is the same situation as in all cases of self-defence. To revisit the hostage example, the hostage-taker's gun might in fact be empty, yet it is still permissible to shoot. As with any decision, we must decide on the best evidence at the time.

Torture in order to save an innocent person is the only situation where it is clearly justifiable. This means that the recent high-profile incidents of torture, apparently undertaken as punitive measures or in a bid to acquire information where there was no evidence of an immediate risk to the life of an innocent person, were reprehensible.

Taking Responsibility

Will a real-life situation actually occur where the only option is between torturing a wrongdoer or saving an innocent person? Perhaps not. However, a minor alteration to the Douglas Wood [an Australian engineer held hostage in Iraq in 2005] situation illustrates that the issue is far from moot. If Western forces in Iraq arrested one of Mr Wood's captors, it would be a perverse ethic that required us to respect the physical integrity of the captor, and not torture him to ascertain Mr Wood's whereabouts, in preference to taking all possible steps to save Mr Wood.

Even if a real-life situation where torture is justifiable does not eventuate, the above argument in favour of torture in limited circumstances needs to be made because it will encourage the community to think more carefully about moral judgements we collectively hold that are the cause of an enormous amount of suffering in the world.

First, no right or interest is absolute. Secondly, rights must always yield to consequences, which are the ultimate criteria upon which the soundness of a decision is gauged. Lost lives hurt a lot more than bent principles.

Thirdly, we must take responsibility not only for the things that we do, but also for the things that we can—but fail to—prevent. The retort that we are not responsible for the lives lost through a decision not to torture a wrongdoer because we did not create the situation is code for moral indifference.

Equally vacuous is the claim that we in the affluent West have no responsibility for more than 13,000 people dying daily due to starvation. Hopefully, the debate on torture will prompt us to correct some of these fundamental failings.

Torture Is Moral When Inflicted for a Greater Good

Patrick J. Buchanan

Patrick J. Buchanan was twice a candidate for the Republican presidential nomination and the Reform Party's candidate in 2000. He is also an author, a founder and editor of The American Conservative *magazine, a political analyst for* MSNBC, *and a syndicated columnist.*

Can torture—the infliction of intolerable, even excruciating, pain to extract information from war criminals—ever be justified?

Civilized society has answered in the negative. No, never. And torture is everywhere outlawed. Regimes that resort to it deny it, lest they be judged barbarous. Routine torture marks the regime that uses it as unworthy of rule or even respect. And rightly so.

Moral Law and Torture

But that does not address the moral question, a question that has arisen with the capture of [Al Qaeda terrorist] Khalid Sheikh Mohammed. Among the crimes to which this monster has been linked are the plot to blow up a dozen airliners over the Pacific, the truck-bomb massacre at the U.S. embassies in Africa, 9/11 [terrorist attacks on the United States] and slashing the throat of [American journalist] Daniel Pearl.

When Mohammed was seized in Pakistan, found with him was a treasure trove for CIA [Central Intelligence Agency] and FBI [Federal Bureau of Investigation] investigators: a computer, disks, tapes and cell phones with data pointing to planned new atrocities.

Patrick J. Buchanan, "The Case for Torture," *World Net Daily*, March 10, 2003. www. worldnetdaily.com. © 2008 Creators Syndicate, Inc. Reproduced by permission.

Mohammed is not talking. Yet, if he can be forced to talk, the information could save thousands. It was said to be two weeks of torture that broke the al-Qaida conspirator who betrayed the plot to blow up those airliners. And if ever there was a case for torture, this excuse for a human being, Khalid Sheikh Mohammed, is it.

The higher law, the moral law, the Natural Law permits ... [torture] in extraordinary circumstances.

Thus, the question: Would it be moral to inflict pain on this beast to force him to reveal what he knows? Positive law prohibits it. However, the higher law, the moral law, the Natural Law permits it in extraordinary circumstances such as these.

Here is the reasoning. The morality of any act depends not only on its character, but on the circumstances and motive. Stealing is wrong and illegal, but stealing food for one's starving family is a moral act. Even killing is not always wrong. If a U.S. soldier had shot Mohammed to save 50 hostages, he would be an American hero.

Fuzzy Thinking

But if it is permissible to take Mohammed's life to save lives, why is it impermissible to inflict pain on him to save lives?

Is the deliberate infliction of pain always immoral? Of course not. Twisting another kid's arm to make him tell where he hid your stolen bicycle is not wrong. Parents spank children to punish them and drive home the lessons of living good lives. Even the caning of that American kid in Singapore that caused a firestorm was not immoral.

Civil War doctors who amputated limbs without anesthesia on battlefields inflicted horrible pain. Why? For a higher good: to save the soldier's life, lest he die of gangrene.

But if doctors can cut off limbs and open up hearts to save lives, and cops may shoot criminals to save lives, and the state may execute criminals, why cannot we commit a lesser evil—squeezing the truth out of Mohammed—for a far greater good: preventing the murder of innocents?

Before America had its vast prison system, petty criminals were locked in stocks in the town square as humiliation. Others were flogged. Barbaric, we now say. But was flogging immoral?

While the instant recoiling that decent people exhibit to the idea of torturing [terrorists] ... may mark them as progressive, it may also be a sign of fuzzy liberal thinking.

Today, many believe that public caning of young criminals, and their return to society for a second chance, would be far better for them and us. It might be a superior deterrent to crime than dumping them into the animal cages that are too many of American prisons, where young offenders face sexual abuse and are exposed to the daily example of how incorrigible criminals succeed and fail.

Who would not prefer a thrashing that might even put one in a hospital for a week to spending years in such a prison?

In short, while the instant recoiling that decent people exhibit to the idea of torturing Mohammed may mark them as progressive, it may also be a sign of fuzzy liberal thinking.

Many of these same folks are all for war on Iraq. Why? To rid the Middle East of a tyrant and his weapons of mass destruction. When [Pope] John Paul II argues that, with inspections underway, such war does not seem necessary, or thus moral, [White House Press Secretary] Ari Fleischer instructed the Holy Father that this war has to be fought to keep Saddam from giving horrible weapons to terrorists.

But if it is moral to go to war and kill thousands to prevent potential acts of terror on U.S. soil, why cannot we inflict pain on one man, if that would stop imminent acts of terror on U.S. soil? There is no evidence Saddam has murdered Americans, but there is a computer full that Mohammed has and has hatched plots to slaughter more.

What will history say about people who hold [President] Harry Truman to be a moral hero for dropping atom bombs on Hiroshima and Nagasaki, but recoil in horror from painfully extracting the truth out of one mass murderer to stop the almost certain slaughter of their own people?

Coercion at Guantánamo Is Not Torture and Is Necessary

Aryeh Spero

Aryeh Spero is a radio talk show host, a weekly columnist for Human Events Online, *and president of Caucus for America, a conservative advocacy organization.*

L ike Freddy Krueger, the anti-Western monsters of the so-called human rights groups reappear every month or so proclaiming: "I'm back!" Their mission is to derail our attempts at defending ourselves against jihadism by demanding impossibly high and foolish standards from America and Israel as to what is allowable in fighting terror while overlooking the daily atrocities by Islamic radicals against the West. Listening to them, one comes away believing that the only place in the world where torture is taking place is at Gitmo [U.S. detention facility in Guantánamo Bay, Cuba] and that the only victims today of cruelty are Islamic terrorists and the "peace-loving" crowds in the Arab street.

Coercion Not Torture

What is happening at Gitmo is not torture but coercion. And it is happening to only those few who we believe have knowledge of impending terrorist strikes against our cities and population or know of others who are formulating such plans. Unlike what is happening in the Islamic and Palestinian world, we Americans do not torture for sheer barbaric enjoyment, or as a means of revenge, nor even as a way of frightening foes. We employ momentary and isolated acts of physical or psychological coercion for the exclusive purpose of eliciting information we are convinced will save lives, thousands of lives.

In the Muslim world, victims are left with permanent defacing of the human body such as cut off fingers, ears, noses, gouged out eyes, and scars and incinerations from fire that remain with the victim for life. Such torture is done for the sake of torture and suffering alone and does not end until the thug reaches self-satisfaction. Such tortures incapacitate and cause excruciating pain for the remainder of that person's life. We do not do any of that.

We carefully have chosen forms of minimal coercion that do not permanently deface and whose duration and effect are limited.

The psychological torture of victims watching their family members writhe in unspeakable pain or death is the enemy's way, not ours. We carefully have chosen forms of minimal coercion that do not permanently deface and whose duration and effect are limited to that moment necessary to convince the terrorist to reveal diabolical schemes. While serious interrogation must be done, we still treat prisoners as human beings while the enemy does everything possible and imaginable to cause needless suffering and strip the persons of humanhood.

What they do is torture, and it is done not to save lives but simply as acts of cruelty. Left-wing scoffers notwithstanding, we have not become like the enemy; we remain in a category eons above that practiced and preached by the jihadists. The anti-Western leftists are simplistic when equating acts of temporary and limited coercion in service of saving lives with those of brutal, open-ended tortures of the worst kind done simply for the sake of agony. They make these simplistic equivalences to demoralize us and shake our belief in the morality and urgency of our cause. We cannot allow the anti-American left within to redefine terms so that that which is not the same is perceived to be the same.

Justifiable Pain

There can be no doubt that the temporary discomfort inflicted upon a particular terrorist is justifiable when done to save thousands. Certainly, pain is not the equivalent of life itself, so that even saving one life takes precedence over the pain of the terrorist. Moreover, we must choose the life of the innocent over the condition of the guilty, especially when the innocent have no recourse whereas the guilty has the option of preventing his own pain by revealing his plans for murder and freely choosing to forgo his plans to kill others. Unlike the innocent American citizen, the terrorist has a way out.

A moral society does not stand by, doing nothing, while an innocent person is about to be killed. It is our moral duty to stop those intent on killing innocent people, or those complicit and knowing of others who wish to kill, before the murder takes place. The "dignity" of the would-be murderer, his treatment, must be inconsequential to those in position to stop him. Indeed, by stopping the terrorist, through coercion, before he murders, we are saving the would-be murderer himself from the sin of murder.

Alas, what is so striking, now, about these left-wing groups is their amorality, their comfort with it. Human Rights Watch and Center for Constitutional Rights have become misnomers for groups preoccupied with the sensibilities of jihadist terrorists.

Misguided Liberals

Normal people understand their obligation to first protect and be concerned about the lives and safety of those for whom they are responsible: first, your family, then your community and nation. Long ago, it became evident that the transnationalists at the *New York Times* and the ACLU [American Civil Liberties Union] are psychologically abnormal and thus do not root for the lives of their countrymen over the lives or even the sensibilities of our enemies. After all, to them, many conservative Americans are the enemy, and those abroad wishing to punish us are kindred spirits.

Alas, what is so striking, now, about these left-wing groups is their amorality, their comfort with it. Human Rights Watch and Center for Constitutional Rights have become misnomers for groups preoccupied with the sensibilities of jihadist terrorists hell-bent on killing innocent Americans yet completely unmoved about the horrific torture of American servicemen and kidnapped Israeli soldiers. They've spent the . . . [first two weeks of January 2007] using contributions from naïve donors to mourn the hanging of Saddam Hussein [on December 30, 2006]. How safe we must all feel knowing they are watching out for the human rights of terrorists and making sure Islamists are provided more constitutional protections than they are willing to grant our President, the Commander in chief.

From the *New York Times*' five-day lament of how Saddam was treated to the obsession of the so-called human rights organizations regarding the need for Club Med amenities at Club Gitmo, it is clear that the left is not liberal or simply misguided. Their perverse politics and view of life have made them amoral. Worse, they have chosen the side of evil. They are no longer respectable company. Their opinions shouldn't matter.

CHAPTER 3

Is Torture an Effective Interrogation Technique?

Chapter Preface

In April 2004, Americans were shocked when photographs were broadcast in the media of Iraqi prisoners being held in Abu Ghraib prison, a U.S. detention facility in Iraq. The photos showed Iraqi prisoners, many stripped naked, many with hoods over their heads, either in stress positions that could cause great pain or in positions designed to be embarrassing or humiliating. Many of the photos also pictured U.S. soldiers standing nearby smiling. The photographs created a scandal in the United States and around the world because quite a few viewers and commentators saw the treatment of the Abu Ghraib prisoners as torture—something that the United States says it does not do. After all, the United States is a signatory to various international agreements prohibiting torture, including the Geneva Conventions, which prohibit all forms of torture or mistreatment of prisoners of war.

At the time of the Abu Ghraib scandal, members of the George W. Bush administration dismissed the photos as abuses perpetrated by a small number of soldiers in violation of U.S. policy. As years passed, however, most experts have come to believe that top administration officials sanctioned or otherwise permitted numerous painful or degrading interrogation techniques as part of the war on terror. The administration has called these "enhanced" interrogation techniques, but they are widely viewed as torture by both experts and lay persons.

Many of these enhanced interrogation techniques have now been documented. In 2007, for example, a U.S. Federal Bureau of Investigation (FBI) report surfaced as part of a lawsuit revealing twenty-six incidents in which detainees at U.S. facilities in Guantánamo Bay, Cuba, were mistreated by U.S. interrogators. According to this report, detainees' hands and feet were shackled to the floor for eighteen hours at a time, causing them to urinate and defecate on themselves. Others had their mouths taped shut with duct tape, with the tape placed over long hair and beards, which would have been painful to remove. Additionally, air conditioning was either turned up or down by interrogators, subjecting detainees to temperature extremes ranging from close to freezing to temperatures over 100 degrees Fahrenheit (38 degrees Celsius). Other incidents included a variety of religious and cultural tactics designed to humiliate and degrade detainees. For example, interrogators interrupted prisoners' prayers and kicked, squatted over, stood on, and sprayed urine on the Koran, the holy book in the Islam religion. And, in a 2006 radio interview, Vice President Dick Cheney explicitly endorsed waterboarding—a technique that simulates drowning—and implied that it was used on the alleged 9/11 mastermind Khalid Sheikh Mohammed at Guantánamo Bay. As reported by *The Guardian* newspaper in an October 27, 2006 article, Cheney called the use of waterboarding on Mohammed a "no-brainer."

The prisoner abuse at Abu Ghraib prison was even better documented. . . .These abuses included actions such as punching, slapping, and kicking detainees, as well as forcing detainees to remove their clothing and keeping them naked for several days at a time.

The prisoner abuse at Abu Ghraib prison was even better documented. In addition to the published photos, other photos and videos taken at the prison were revealed by the Pentagon to lawmakers in a private meeting on May 12, 2004. Although these photos were never released to the public, they reportedly depicted dogs snarling at prisoners, women forced to expose their breasts at gunpoint, and prisoners forced to perform sexual and homosexual acts. Also in 2004, the U.S. Army conducted an investigation and issued the *Taguba Report*, which documented abuse of the Abu Ghraib detainees. Reporter Seymour M. Hersh relied on the government report as a source for a May 2004 article in *The New Yorker* magazine that exposed the abuses in detail. These abuses included actions such as punching, slapping, and kicking detainees, as well as forcing detainees to remove their clothing and keeping them naked for several days at a time. Captors also videotaped and photographed naked male and female detainees in sexually explicit positions, forced naked male detainees to wear women's underwear, and forced groups of male detainees to commit sexual acts while being photographed and videotaped. In at least one case, a naked detainee was made to stand on a box, with a sandbag on his head and wires attached to his fingers, toes, and genitals to threaten electric torture. In other cases, dogs without muzzles were used to intimidate and frighten (and, in at least one case, bite and injure) Arab prisoners, who tend to have a cultural fear of dogs. In follow-up reports, *The New York Times* reported additional abuse at Abu Ghraib, including urinating on detainees, jumping on and pounding on a detainee's wounded leg, pouring phosphoric acid on detainees, and more sexual abuse.

There is also evidence that these techniques were used by U.S. interrogators in other locations. On February 7, 2008, in testimony before the Senate Select Intelligence Committee, Director of Central Intelligence Mike Hayden admitted that the Central Intelligence Agency (CIA) used "enhanced interrogation" at the CIA's "black sites"—secret prisons operated by the agency to interrogate suspected terrorists.

Despite the public outrage over use of these methods, the Bush administration has stood firm in defending enhanced interrogation techniques. In March 2008, for example, President Bush vetoed legislation that would have banned many harsh interrogation techniques such as waterboarding. As reported by The Associated Press on March 8, 2008, President Bush called these techniques "the most valuable tools in the war on terror" and "practices that have a proven track record of keeping America safe."

Whether these or other even harsher interrogation techniques are actually effective in acquiring useful intelligence information, however, is one of the most debated issues in the dialogue about torture. The viewpoints in this chapter explore this critical issue.

Torture Is Sometimes Effective

Alan M. Dershowitz

Alan M. Dershowitz is a lawyer, author, political commentator, and professor of law at Harvard Law School.

Most Americans—Democrats, Republicans, independents or undecided—want a president who will be strong, as well as smart, on national security, and who will do everything in his or her lawful power to prevent further acts of terrorism.

Hundreds of thousands of Americans may watch [liberal filmmaker] Michael Moore's movies or cheer [war protester] Cindy Sheehan's demonstrations, but tens of millions want the Moores and Sheehans of our nation as far away as possible from influencing national security policy. . . .

The Ticking Bomb Scenario

Consider, for example, the contentious and emotionally laden issue of the use of torture in securing preventive intelligence information about imminent acts of terrorism—the so-called "ticking bomb" scenario. I am not now talking about the routine use of torture in interrogation of suspects or the humiliating misuse of sexual taunting that infamously occurred at Abu Ghraib [a U.S. detention facility in Iraq]. I am talking about that rare situation described by former President [Bill] Clinton in an interview with National Public Radio:

> You picked up someone you know is the No. 2 aide to Osama bin Laden. And you know they have an operation planned for the United States or some European capital in the next three days. And you know this guy knows it. Right, that's the clearest example. And you think you can only get

Alan M. Dershowitz, "Democrats and Waterboarding," *The Wall Street Journal*, November 7, 2007. www.opinionjournal.com. Reprinted with permission of *The Wall Street Journal*.

it out of this guy by shooting him full of some drugs or waterboarding him or otherwise working him over.

Any president . . . would in fact authorize some forms of torture against a captured terrorist if . . . this was the only way . . . to prevent an imminent mass casualty attack.

He said Congress should draw a narrow statute "which would permit the president to make a finding in a case like I just outlined, and then that finding could be submitted even if after the fact to the Foreign Intelligence Surveillance Court." The president would have to "take personal responsibility" for authorizing torture in such an extreme situation. Sen. John McCain [Republican presidential nominee] has also said that as president he would take responsibility for authorizing torture in that "one in a million" situation.

Although I am personally opposed to the use of torture, I have no doubt that any president—indeed any leader of a democratic nation—would in fact authorize some forms of torture against a captured terrorist if he believed that this was the only way of securing information necessary to prevent an imminent mass casualty attack. The only dispute is whether he would do so openly with accountability or secretly with deniability. The former seems more consistent with democratic theory, the latter with typical political hypocrisy.

There are some who claim that torture is a nonissue because it never works—it only produces false information. This is simply not true, as evidenced by the many decent members of the French Resistance who, under Nazi torture, disclosed the locations of their closest friends and relatives.

The kind of torture that President Clinton was talking about is not designed to secure confessions of past crimes, but rather to obtain real time, actionable intelligence deemed necessary to prevent an act of mass casualty terrorism. The question put to the captured terrorist is not "Did you do it?" Instead, the suspect is asked to disclose self-proving information, such as the location of the bomber.

As a matter of constitutional law . . . the issue of "waterboarding" cannot be decided in the abstract.

Recently, Israeli security officials confronted a ticking-bomb situation. Several days before Yom Kippur, they received credible information that a suicide bomber was planning to blow himself up in a crowded synagogue on the holiest day of the Jewish year. After a gun battle in which an Israeli soldier was killed, the commander of the terrorist cell in Nablus [a Palestinian city] was captured. Interrogation led to the location of the suicide bomb in a Tel Aviv apartment. Israel denies that it uses torture and I am aware of no evidence that it did so to extract life-saving information in this case.

Water boarding

But what if lawful interrogation failed to uncover the whereabouts of the suicide bomber? What other forms of pressure should be employed in this situation?

Government officials must strike an appropriate balance between the security of America and the rights of our enemies.

This brings us to waterboarding. [U.S. Attorney General] Michael Mukasey is absolutely correct, as a matter of constitutional law, that the issue of "waterboarding" cannot be decided in the abstract. Under prevailing precedents—some of which I disagree with—the court must examine the nature of the governmental interest at stake, and the degree to which the government actions at issue shock the conscience, and then decide on a case-by-case basis. In several cases involving actions at least as severe as waterboarding, courts have found no violations of due process.

The members of the judiciary committee who voted against Judge Mukasey, because of his unwillingness to support an absolute prohibition on waterboarding and all other forms of torture, should be asked the direct question: Would you authorize the use of waterboarding, or other non-lethal forms of torture, if you believed that it was the only possible way of saving the lives of hundreds of Americans in a situation of the kind faced by Israeli authorities on the eve of Yom Kippur? Would you want your president to authorize extraordinary means of interrogation in such a situation? If so, what means? If not, would you be prepared to accept responsibility for the preventable deaths of hundreds of Americans?

Perhaps political campaigns and confirmation hearings are not the appropriate fora in which to conduct subtle and difficult debates about tragic choices that a president or attorney general may face. But nor are they the appropriate settings for hypocritical public posturing by political figures who, in private, would almost certainly opt for torture if they believed it was necessary to save numerous American lives. What is needed is a recognition that government officials must strike an appropriate balance between the security of America and the rights of our enemies.

Torture Has a Place in the War on Terror

Nicholas Davis

Nicholas Davis attended Texas A&M University and contributed articles to the school's student newspaper, The Battalion.

Information is crucial. Anyone will admit this, be it a businessman or a soldier. Successful businesses are dependent on the best information available, and wars are won in a similar fashion. This brings us to a crossroad. During a war, how far should one go to extract information from a prisoner? Is torture ever justifiable? In some cases, it is.

Denying the Use of Torture

Recently, some documents prepared by defense department lawyers and the president's [George W. Bush] legal advisors have surfaced, instructing the president on ways to get around torture laws.

Of course, many individuals believe this is a crime against humanity and a breach of American and international law. However, torture may indeed play a key role in protecting U.S. soldiers and this nation.

Still, the Bush administration has tried to downplay and even deny that the president has ordered the use of torture.

[President] Bush has stooped to playing such word games because he realizes torture is indeed useful, and in some instances necessary.

For example, [former Attorney General] John Ashcroft, in a testimony to the Senate Judiciary Committee, stated, "Presi-

Nicholas Davis, "Making a Case for Torture: Finding Ways Around Torture Legislation a Good Move in Ending War on Terror," *The Battalion*, June 17, 2004. http://media. www.thebatt.com. Reproduced by permission.

dent Bush made no order that would require or direct the violation of either international treaties or domestic laws prohibiting torture."

Last week [early June 2004], however, the *Wall Street Journal* broke the story of a classified legal brief to [former] Secretary [of Defense] Donald Rumsfeld regarding the difficulties interrogators faced in obtaining information from prisoners.

The brief stated, "because the president is protecting national security, any ban on torture, even an American Law, could not be approved."

Basically, this implies that the president's charter to protect national security trumps the laws of torture.

Other memorandums pertain to using harsh interrogation techniques while side-stepping the classification of torture.

One such memorandum, reported by *The New York Times*, claimed "a defendant is guilty of torture only if he acts with the express purpose of inflicting severe pain or suffering on a person within his control."

Bush claims he ordered interrogators to use methods compatible with international and American law, but it's obvious that a word game is being played. That is, what constitutes "severe pain" is completely circumstantial.

Most likely, Bush has stooped to playing such word games because he realizes torture is indeed useful, and in some instances necessary. Nevertheless, he also understands that many American voters live in a constant state of idealism and naivete and would not reelect a man who advocates torture.

Torture Needed in the War on Terror

Unfortunately these people fail to see the big picture.

Remember these "enemy combatants" fight for no national standing army and have no rights under the Geneva Conventions [a series of international treaties governing the treatment of prisoners of war]. More importantly, since these individuals fight for no standing army, it is obvious they are motivated by something more than nationalism: A sick ideology inspired by a religious theology.

These terrorists believe they fight for God, so it is nearly impossible to obtain vital information quickly. After all, it's easy to squeal on your government, but not God. This is why more persuasion is needed.

The international community and many delusional people here in the United States believe that Americans should treat the terrorists held as prisoners in a humane and delicate fashion. Why is this?

The harsh truth is torture has a place in the war on terror, especially since nuclear weapons are more accessible.

The reason offered is, "If Americans torture prisoners, then the enemy will torture American POWs [prisoners of war]."

This is the most important point. Nevertheless, it fails to hold water. To explain, it seems that only Americans and their allies hold themselves to the standards of the treaties regarding prisoner treatment. Does anyone believe our soldiers held as POWs in Korea, Vietnam, the Gulf War or the Iraq War were treated in such a fashion? Absolutely not.

It's terrible that torture should even be considered as an option, but Americans must ask themselves, "How much longer should this war on terror continue. How many more innocent lives need to be lost?"

Without question, torture is inhumane, but wake up. These terrorists must not be pampered. They should be so terrified when captured that they are willing to tell interrogators anything they want to know.

Admittedly, this method can be viewed as cruel, but so can suicide bombings targeting innocent civilians and children, flying airplanes into buildings or dragging the body parts of Americans down the streets of Fallujah [a town in Iraq].

The harsh truth is torture has a place in the war on terror, especially since nuclear weapons are more accessible. If prisoners are unwilling to relinquish vital information that may save a few American lives or an entire city by thwarting a nuclear attack, then our interrogators should have no reservations about starting at the prisoners' toes and working their way up.

Torture Works as a Social Control

Naomi Klein

*Naomi Klein is an award-winning journalist, syndicated colum-
nist, and best-selling author.*

I recently caught a glimpse of the effects of torture in action
at an event honoring Maher Arar. The Syrian-born Canadian is the world's most famous victim of "rendition," the
process by which US officials outsource torture to foreign
countries. Arar was switching planes in New York when US
interrogators detained him and "rendered" him to Syria, where
he was held for ten months in a cell slightly larger than a
grave and taken out periodically for beatings.

Arar was being honored for his courage by the Canadian
Council on American-Islamic Relations, a mainstream advocacy organization. The audience gave him a heartfelt standing
ovation, but there was fear mixed in with the celebration.
Many of the prominent community leaders kept their distance
from Arar, responding to him only tentatively. Some speakers
were unable even to mention the honored guest by name, as if
he had something they could catch. And perhaps they were
right: The tenuous "evidence"—later discredited—that landed
Arar in a rat-infested cell was guilt by association. And if that
could happen to Arar, a successful software engineer and family man, who is safe?

In a rare public speech, Arar addressed this fear directly.
He told the audience that an independent commissioner has
been trying to gather evidence of law-enforcement officials
breaking the rules when investigating Muslim Canadians. The
commissioner has heard dozens of stories of threats, harass-

Naomi Klein, "Torture's Dirty Secret: It Works," *The Nation*, May 30, 2005. www.the
nation.com. Reproduced by permission of the author.

ment and inappropriate home visits. But, Arar said, "not a single person made a public complaint. Fear prevented them from doing so." Fear of being the next Maher Arar.

This is torture's true purpose: to terrorize—not only [the detained] . . . but also, and more important, the broader community that hears about these abuses.

Fear Among U.S. Muslims

The fear is even thicker among Muslims in the United States, where the Patriot Act gives police the power to seize the records of any mosque, school, library or community group on mere suspicion of terrorist links. When this intense surveillance is paired with the ever-present threat of torture, the message is clear: You are being watched, your neighbor may be a spy, the government can find out anything about you. If you misstep, you could disappear onto a plane bound for Syria, or into "the deep dark hole that is Guantánamo Bay," to borrow a phrase from Michael Ratner, president of the Center for Constitutional Rights.

But this fear has to be finely calibrated. The people being intimidated need to know enough to be afraid but not so much that they demand justice. This helps explain why the Defense Department will release certain kinds of seemingly incriminating information about Guantánamo—pictures of men in cages, for instance—at the same time that it acts to suppress photographs on a par with what escaped from Abu Ghraib [a U.S. detention facility in Iran]. And it might also explain why the Pentagon approved the new book by a former military translator, including the passages about prisoners being sexually humiliated, but prevented him from writing about the widespread use of attack dogs. This strategic leaking of information, combined with official denials, induces a state of mind that Argentines describe as "knowing/not knowing," a vestige of their "dirty war" [a government campaign against suspected dissidents from 1976 to 1983].

"Obviously, intelligence agents have an incentive to hide the use of unlawful methods," says the ACLU's [American Civil Liberty Union] Jameel Jaffer. "On the other hand, when they use rendition and torture as a threat, it's undeniable that they benefit, in some sense, from the fact that people know that intelligence agents are willing to act unlawfully. They benefit from the fact that people understand the threat and believe it to be credible."

And the threats have been received. In an affidavit filed with an ACLU court challenge to Section 215 of the Patriot Act, Nazih Hassan, president of the Muslim Community Association of Ann Arbor, Michigan, describes this new climate. Membership and attendance are down, donations are way down, board members have resigned—Hassan says his members fear doing anything that could get their names on lists. One member testified anonymously that he has "stopped speaking out on political and social issues" because he doesn't want to draw attention to himself.

Torture continues to be debated in the United States as if it were merely a morally questionable way to extract information, not an instrument of state terror.

The Purpose of Torture

This is torture's true purpose: to terrorize—not only the people in Guantánamo's cages and Syria's isolation cells but also, and more important, the broader community that hears about these abuses. Torture is a machine designed to break the will to resist—the individual prisoner's will and the collective will.

This is not a controversial claim. In 2001 the US NGO [non-governmental organization] Physicians for Human

Rights published a manual on treating torture survivors that noted: "perpetrators often attempt to justify their acts of torture and ill treatment by the need to gather information. Such conceptualizations obscure the purpose of torture. . . . The aim of torture is to dehumanize the victim, break his/her will, and at the same time, set horrific examples for those who come in contact with the victim. In this way, torture can break or damage the will and coherence of entire communities."

Yet despite this body of knowledge, torture continues to be debated in the United States as if it were merely a morally questionable way to extract information, not an instrument of state terror. But there's a problem: No one claims that torture is an effective interrogation tool—least of all the people who practice it. Torture "doesn't work. There are better ways to deal with captives," CIA director Porter Goss told the Senate Intelligence Committee on February 16 [2005]. And a recently declassified memo written by an FBI [Federal Bureau of Investigation] official in Guantánamo states that extreme coercion produced "nothing more than what FBI got using simple investigative techniques." The Army's own interrogation field manual states that force "can induce the source to say whatever he thinks the interrogator wants to hear."

And yet the abuses keep on coming—Uzbekistan as the new hot spot for renditions; the "El Salvador model" imported to Iraq. And the only sensible explanation for torture's persistent popularity comes from a most unlikely source. Lynndie England, the fall girl for Abu Ghraib, was asked during her botched trial why she and her colleagues had forced naked prisoners into a human pyramid. "As a way to control them," she replied.

Exactly. As an interrogation tool, torture is a bust. But when it comes to social control, nothing works quite like torture.

It Is a Myth That Torture Works

Anne Applebaum

Anne Applebaum is a politics and foreign policy columnist for The Washington Post *newspaper.*

Just for a moment, let's pretend that there is no moral, legal or constitutional problem with torture. Let's also imagine a clear-cut case: a terrorist who knows where bombs are about to explode in Iraq. To stop him, it seems that a wide range of Americans would be prepared to endorse "cruel and unusual" methods. In advance of confirmation hearings for [former] Attorney General-designate Alberto Gonzales ... the *Wall Street Journal* argued that such scenarios must be debated, since "what's at stake in this controversy is nothing less than the ability of U.S. forces to interrogate enemies who want to murder innocent civilians." Alan Dershowitz, the liberal legal scholar, has argued in the past that interrogators in such a case should get a "torture warrant" from a judge. Both of these arguments rest on an assumption: that torture—defined as physical pressure during interrogation—can be used to extract useful information.

Does Torture Work?

But does torture work? The question has been asked many times since Sept. 11, 2001. I'm repeating it, however, because the Gonzales hearings inspired more articles about our lax methods ... and because I still cannot find a positive answer. I've heard it said that the Syrians and the Egyptians "really know how to get these things done." I've heard the Israelis mentioned, without proof. I've heard Algeria mentioned, too but Darius Rejali, an academic who recently trolled through French archives, found no clear examples of how torture helped the French in Algeria—and they lost that war anyway. "Liberals," argued an article in the liberal online magazine *Slate* a few months ago, "have a tendency to accept, all too eagerly, the argument that torture is ineffective." But it's also true that "realists," whether liberal or conservative, have a tendency to accept, all too eagerly, fictitious accounts of effective torture carried out by someone else.

Nine out of 10 people can be persuaded to talk with no "stress methods" at all, let alone cruel and unusual ones.

By contrast, it is easy to find experienced U.S. officers who argue precisely the opposite. Meet, for example, retired Air Force Col. John Rothrock, who, as a young captain, headed a combat interrogation team in Vietnam. More than once he was faced with a ticking time-bomb scenario: a captured Vietcong guerrilla who knew of plans to kill Americans. What was done in such cases was "not nice," he says. "But we did not physically abuse them." Rothrock used psychology, the shock of capture and of the unexpected. Once, he let a prisoner see a wounded comrade die. Yet—as he remembers saying to the "desperate and honorable officers" who wanted him to move faster—"if I take a Bunsen burner to the guy's genitals, he's going to tell you just about anything," which would be pointless. Rothrock, who is no squishy liberal, says that he doesn't know "any professional intelligence officers of my generation who would think this is a good idea."

Or listen to Army Col. Stuart Herrington, a military intelligence specialist who conducted interrogations in Vietnam, Panama and Iraq during Desert Storm, and who was sent by the Pentagon in 2003—long before Abu Ghraib—to assess interrogations in Iraq. Aside from its immorality and its illegality, says Herrington, torture is simply "not a good way to get information." In his experience, nine out of 10 people can be persuaded to talk with no "stress methods" at all, let alone cruel and unusual ones. Asked whether that would be true of religiously motivated fanatics, he says that the "batting average" might be lower: "perhaps six out of ten." And if you beat up the remaining four? "They'll just tell you anything to get you to stop."

Side Effects of Torture

Worse, you'll have the other side effects of torture. It "endangers our soldiers on the battlefield by encouraging reciprocity." It does "damage to our country's image" and undermines our credibility in Iraq. That, in the long run, outweighs any theoretical benefit. Herrington's confidential Pentagon report, which he won't discuss but which was leaked to *The Post* a month ago, goes farther. In that document, he warned that members of an elite military and CIA [Central Intelligence Agency] task force were abusing detainees in Iraq, that their activities could be "making gratuitous enemies" and that prisoner abuse "is counterproductive to the Coalition's efforts to win the cooperation of the Iraqi citizenry." Far from rescuing Americans, in other words, the use of "special methods" might help explain why the war is going so badly.

Given the overwhelmingly negative evidence, the really interesting question is . . . why so many people in our society want to believe that . . . [torture] works.

An up-to-date illustration of the colonel's point appeared in recently released FBI [Federal Bureau of Investigation] documents from the naval base at Guantanamo Bay, Cuba. These show, among other things, that some military intelligence officers wanted to use harsher interrogation methods than the FBI did. As a result, complained one inspector, "every time the FBI established a rapport with a detainee, the military would step in and the detainee would stop being cooperative." So much for the utility of torture.

Given the overwhelmingly negative evidence, the really interesting question is not whether torture works but why so many people in our society want to believe that it works. At the moment, there is a myth in circulation, a fable that goes something like this: Radical terrorists will take advantage of our fussy legality, so we may have to suspend it to beat them. Radical terrorists mock our namby-pamby prisons, so we must make them tougher. Radical terrorists are nasty, so to defeat them we have to be nastier.

Perhaps it's reassuring to tell ourselves tales about the new forms of "toughness" we need, or to talk about the special rules we will create to defeat this special enemy. Unfortunately, that toughness is self-deceptive and self-destructive. Ultimately it will be self-defeating as well.

Torture Is Neither Justified Nor Effective

Mick Smith

Mick (Michael) Smith is an investigative journalist from Britain who writes on defense and intelligence matters for the British newspaper The Sunday Times. *He also is the author of a number of best-selling books.*

Concern over the arbitrary way in which the US administration attempts to justify its abuse of prisoners ... [in] Guantanamo Bay [a U.S. detention facility in Cuba] had eased recently with clear signs that under pressure from its allies, and in particular Britain, the White House was looking to find a way to get rid of the Guantanamo problem. But it is now clear such optimism was misplaced.

The Pentagon has decided that a new army interrogation manual on the use of torture won't include a key tenet of the Geneva Conventions [international treaties governing the treatment of prisoners of war], that prisoners should not be subject to "humiliating and degrading treatment". Military lawyers had attempted to make Article 3 of the conventions, which covers this issue, a key part of the manual in an attempt to prevent a recurrence of the abuses meted out to Iraqi prisoners at Abu Ghraib [a U.S. detention facility in Iraq].

But [former Vice President] Dick Cheney and [former Secretary of Defense] Donald Rumsfeld intervened, through their sidekicks David Addington, the vice-president's chief of staff, and Stephen Cambone, Rumsfeld's protégée and defense under-secretary for intelligence. Their argument was that including a clause banning "humiliating and degrading treat-

Mick Smith, "Torture Is Neither Justified Nor Effective," *Timesonline*, June 6, 2006. http://timesonline.typepad.com. Reproduced by permission.

ment" would restrict America's ability to question detainees. Yes. I know. That's the whole point. But in an atmosphere where senior officials think anything goes it is perhaps unsurprising that scandals such as Abu Ghraib occur. It might even be argued that the alleged massacre at Haditha can be traced back to this "anything goes" attitude from on high.

The Bush administration has performed a series of somersaults in its attempts to show that it "does not torture" prisoners.

The [George W.] Bush Administration's Torture Definitions

The Bush administration has performed a series of somersaults in its attempts to show that it "does not torture" prisoners, carefully articulating its own definition of what is and is not torture. In August 2002, the Department of Justice issued a memo which said that the Geneva Conventions preventing interrogators inflicting "severe pain" only referred to pain "equivalent in intensity to the pain accompanying serious physical injury, such as organ failure, impairment of bodily function, or even death." It added that "humiliating and degrading treatment" was only such if it caused long-term psychological damage to the victim.

This provided a wonderful Catch-22 situation of course. Unless the prisoner died, he could not be subject to "severe pain" and since there was no way of knowing if any "humiliating and degrading treatment" was causing long-term psychological damage, the prisoner could effectively be subjected to any form of humiliating and degrading treatment until the point where he became a gibbering wreck.

That memo was eventually withdrawn, in December 2004. But between August 2002 and December 2004 it was the official position of the US administration that it could administer both "severe pain" and "humiliating and degrading treatment" to prisoners so long as they did not die and remained sane. Last week, an Army dog handler became the 11th US soldier to be convicted in relation to the Abu Ghraib scandal, in which Iraqi prisoners were subjected to humiliating treatment during late 2003 and early 2004. You will not however see any Department of Justice officials in the dock.

Almost anyone will eventually talk when subjected to enough physical pressures, but the information obtained in this way is likely to be of little intelligence value.

The August 2002 Department of Justice memo at least placed a limit of sorts on the use of "humiliating and degrading treatment". The new Army interrogation manual does not even do that. But rest assured that when a prisoner is sent insane by such treatment Messrs Addington and Cambone, and for that matter Cheney and Rumsfeld, will be perfectly safe from prosecution.

The Value of Torture

There will be some of course who will argue that such methods are justified in the new war we are fighting, the war on terror, or the Long War as it is now apparently known. Any means of getting terrorists to talk is justified in order to get the intelligence we need. Well by coincidence, just as the Pentagon was reaffirming that it doesn't need to worry about the niceties of the Geneva Convention, the CIA [Central Intelligence Agency] was releasing a 1996 interrogation manual, which states:

"The question of torture should be disposed of at once. Quite apart from moral and legal considerations, physical torture or extreme mental torture is not an expedient device. Maltreating the subject is from a strictly practical point of view as short-sighted as whipping a horse to his knees before a thirty-mile ride. It is true that almost anyone will eventually talk when subjected to enough physical pressures, but the information obtained in this way is likely to be of little intelligence value."

Torture Ruins Evidence that Could Be Used to Prosecute Terrorists

Phillip Carter

Phillip Carter is a former Army officer who writes on legal and military affairs from Los Angeles.

There are plenty of good reasons to avoid using torture in interrogations. It's an immoral and barbaric practice condemned by most Western nations and theological traditions, for starters. International human rights law and U.S. criminal law both outlaw it. And as if that's not enough, there is serious doubt as to whether torture even produces reliable intelligence, as Mark Bowden explains in the October 2003 issue of the *Atlantic Monthly*.

Add this additional reason to the list: Any information gained through torture will almost certainly be excluded from court in any criminal prosecution of the tortured defendant. And, to make matters worse for federal prosecutors, the use of torture to obtain statements may make those statements (and any evidence gathered as a result of those statements) inadmissible in the trials of other defendants as well. Thus, the net effect of torture is to undermine the entire federal law enforcement effort to put terrorists behind bars. With each alleged terrorist we torture, we most likely preclude the possibility of a criminal trial for him, and for any of the confederates he may incriminate.

Thanks to a report in Wednesday's *New York Times*, we now know that the United States has intentionally used (with the sanction of the highest levels of government) torture tactics to pry open the mind of Khalid Sheik Mohammed, alleged to be one of al-Qaida's top masterminds. According to the *Times*, "C.I.A. interrogators used graduated levels of force, including a technique known as 'water boarding,' in which a prisoner is strapped down, forcibly pushed under water and made to believe he might drown." Gen. Peter Pace, the vice chairman of the Joint Chiefs of Staff, described such tactics as a violation of the Geneva Conventions. And the FBI has instructed its agents to steer clear of such coercive interrogation methods, for fear that their involvement might compromise testimony in future criminal cases.

The use of torture during interrogation has so many negative consequences that it may ultimately allow some accused terrorists to win acquittals.

So, setting aside for a moment all the moral, political, and practical problems of such tactics (staggering though these problems may be), as a purely legal matter, the use of torture during interrogation has so many negative consequences that it may ultimately allow some accused terrorists to win acquittals merely because it will lead to suppressed evidence of their factual guilt.

Evidence (such as a confession) gathered as a result of torturing a person like Mohammed will be excluded at *his* trial, if he ever sees one. This is true both in federal courts, which operate under the Federal Rules of Evidence, and military courts, which operate under the Military Rules of Evidence. Both the Fifth Amendment's right against compulsory self-incrimination and the 14th Amendment's guarantee of due process preclude the use of a defendant's coerced statement against him in criminal court. In addition, any evidence gathered because of information learned through torture (sometimes called "derivative evidence") will likely also be excluded. Furthermore, the Supreme Court suggested in its landmark Fifth Amendment case, *Oregon v. Elstad*, that it might exclude evidence gathered after the use of any coercion, regardless of attempts by police and prosecutors to offset the coercion with measures like a *Miranda* warning. If Mohammed were prosecuted, and a court followed the line of reasoning set forth in *Elstad*, he might well see the charges against him evaporate entirely for lack of evidence.

Right now, the Justice Department has no plans to criminally prosecute Mohammed or other top al-Qaida leaders (like Abu Zubaida) currently being held by the United States in shadowy detention facilities overseas. But federal prosecutors have filed charges against alleged al-Qaida member Zacarias Moussaoui for being part of the 9/11 conspiracy. And the Supreme Court is now considering whether trials of some sort are constitutionally required for other alleged terrorists. Problems with the Moussaoui case reflect the problem with evidence obtained through coerced confessions. In that case, it's not the government that seeks to bring in the tortured al-Qaida leaders' out-of-court statements—it's Moussaoui, the defendant. However, the result may be the same. Such out-of-court statements will likely be challenged as hearsay by whatever side isn't trying to bring them into court. And under the applicable hearsay exception, for declarations against interest, such statements are only admissible if they carry certain indicia of reliability. Given the questionable ability of torture to produce reliable information, this will be a hotly contested issue. It's not clear whether this evidence will ever be admitted to court.

This torture of top al-Qaida leaders may also cause problems for the government were there to be a trial for the alleged "dirty bomber" Jose Padilla. The tip that led to Padilla's initial detention on a material witness warrant in May 2002 came from intensive CIA interrogations of Zubaida, a close associate of Osama Bin Laden. In December 2003, the 2nd Circuit Court of Appeals ordered that Padilla be released from military custody and either charged in federal court or released. However, any prosecution of Padilla could be very problematic for the government, because the case for his guilt rests mostly (if not entirely) on secret interrogations of al-Qaida leaders, which now appear to have involved torture. If a criminal case is ever brought against Padilla, his lawyers are sure to challenge this crucial evidence on a number of grounds, including reliability and the fact that it was procured with torture in a way that "shocks the conscience."

In the long run . . . [the U.S. use of torture] will show that we have compromised such liberal, democratic ideals like adherence to the rule of law to counter terrorism.

Interestingly, such problems would not have arisen had these suspects been hauled before a military tribunal at the outset. The Pentagon's procedural rules for tribunals allow evidence to be admitted if it "would have probative value to a reasonable person." These rules contain no provision for the exclusion of involuntary statements, and on their face, do not allow the presiding officer of such tribunals to rely on Supreme Court precedent or federal case law to decide issues of evidence. Presumably, these tribunals were designed to allow for the admission of evidence from dubious circumstances, including the "intensive questioning" of Mohammed and Zubaida. So, if the Pentagon moves forward with its plans to try al-Qaida members before these courts, it may be able to evade this problem altogether.

However, even that won't solve the problem for the rest of the legal system, which only allows evidence obtained through constitutional means. By using torture to question the top terrorists it has in custody, the government has effectively sabotaged any future prosecutions of al-Qaida players—major and minor—that might depend on evidence gathered through those interrogations. It's plausible that skilled interrogation by the FBI, in accordance with American law, could have produced valuable evidence of these terrorists' guilt, which could have been used in court. But now that torture has been used, that may just be wishful hindsight.

As a nation, we still haven't clearly decided whether it's better to prosecute terrorists or pound them with artillery. But by torturing some of al-Qaida's leaders, we have completely undermined any efforts to do the former and irreversibly committed ourselves to a martial plan of justice. In the long run, this may be counterproductive, and it will show that we have compromised such liberal, democratic ideals like adherence to the rule of law to counter terrorism. Torture and tribunals do not help America show that it believes in the rule of law. But if CIA officials continue to use tactics that will get evidence thrown out of federal court, there will increasingly be no other option.

History Shows Torture Does Not Obtain the Truth

Robert Fisk

Robert Fisk is a British journalist and is Middle East correspondent for the British newspaper The Independent.

"Torture works," an American special forces major—now, needless to say, a colonel—boasted to a colleague of mine a couple of years ago. It seems that the CIA and its hired thugs in Afghanistan and Iraq still believe this. There is no evidence that rendition and beatings and waterboarding and the insertion of metal pipes into men' anuses—and, of course, the occasional torturing to death of detainees—has ended. Why else would the CIA admit in January that it had destroyed videotapes of prisoners being almost drowned—the "waterboarding" technique—before they could be seen by US investigators?

Yet only a few days ago, I came across a medieval print in which a prisoner has been strapped to a wooden chair, a leather hosepipe pushed down his throat and a primitive pump fitted at the top of the hose where an ill-clad torturer is hard at work squirting water down the hose. The prisoner's eyes bulge with terror as he feels himself drowning, all the while watched by Spanish inquisitors who betray not the slightest feelings of sympathy with the prisoner. Who said "waterboarding" was new? The Americans are just aping their predecessors in the inquisition.

Another medieval print I found in a Canadian newspaper in November shows a prisoner under interrogation in what I suspect is medieval Germany. In this case, he has been strapped backwards to the outer edge of a wheel. Two hooded men are administering his agony. One is using a bellows to encourage a fire burning at the bottom of the wheel while the other is turning the wheel forwards so that the prisoner's feet are moving into the flames. The eyes of this poor man—naked save for a cloth over his lower torso—are tight shut in pain. Two priests stand beside him, one cowled, the other wearing a robe over his surplice, a paper and pen in hand to take down the prisoner's words.

Anthony Grafton, who has been working on a book about magic in Renaissance Europe, says that in the 16th and 17th centuries, torture was systematically used against anyone suspected of witchcraft, his or her statements taken down by sworn notaries—the equivalent, I suppose, of the CIA's interrogation officers—and witnessed by officials who made no pretence that this was anything other than torture; no talk of "enhanced interrogation" from the lads who turned the wheel to the fire.

Two tortured women managed to exonerate children but eventually, in Grafton's words, "they implicated loved ones, friends and members of other Jewish communities". Thus did torture force innocent civilians to confess to fantastical crimes.

As Grafton recounts, "The pioneering medievalist Henry Charles Lea . . . wrote at length about the ways in which inquisitors had used torture to make prisoners confess heretical views and actions. An enlightened man writing in what he saw as an enlightened age, he looked back in horror at these barbarous practices and condemned them with a clarity that anyone reading public statements must now envy."

There were professionals in the Middle Ages who were trained to use pain as a method of enquiry as well as an ultimate punishment before death. Men who were to be "hanged, drawn and quartered" in medieval London, for example, would be shown the "instruments" before their final suffering began with the withdrawal of their intestines in front of vast crowds of onlookers. Most of those tortured for information in medieval times were anyway executed after they had provided the necessary information to their interrogators. These inquisitions—with details of the torture that accompanied them—were published and disseminated widely so that the public should understand the threat that the prisoners had represented and the power of those who inflicted such pain upon them. No destroying of videotapes here. Illustrated pamphlets and songs, according to Grafton, were added to the repertory of publicity.

Ronnie Po-chia Hsia and Italian scholars Diego Quaglioni and Anna Esposito have studied the 15th-century Trent inquisition whose victims were usually Jews. In 1475, three Jewish households were accused of murdering a Christian boy called Simon to carry out the supposed Passover "ritual" of using his blood to make "matzo" bread. This "blood libel"—it was, of course, a total falsity—is still, alas, believed in many parts of the Middle East although it is frightening to discover that the idea was well established in 15th century Europe.

Torture does not obtain truth. It will make most ordinary people say anything the torturer wants.

As usual, the podestà—a city official—was the interrogator, who regarded external evidence as providing mere clues of guilt. Europe was then still governed by Roman law which required confessions in order to convict. As Grafton describes horrifyingly, once the prisoner's answers no longer satisfied the podestà, the torturer tied the man's or woman's arms behind their back and the prisoner would then be lifted by a pulley, agonisingly, towards the ceiling. "Then, on orders of the podestà, the torturer would make the accused 'jump' or 'dance'—pulling him or her up, then releasing the rope, dislocating limbs and inflicting stunning pain."

When a member of one of the Trent Jewish families, Samuel, asked the podestà where he had heard that Jews needed Christian blood, the interrogator replied—and all this while, it should be remembered, Samuel was dangling in the air on the pulley—that he had heard it from other Jews. Samuel said that he was being tortured unjustly. "The truth, the truth!" the podestà shouted, and Samuel was made to "jump" up to eight feet, telling his interrogator: "God the Helper and truth help me." After 40 minutes, he was returned to prison.

Once broken, the Jewish prisoners, of course, confessed. After another torture session, Samuel named a fellow Jew. Further sessions of torture finally broke him and he invented the Jewish ritual murder plot and named others guilty of this non-existent crime. Two tortured women managed to exonerate children but eventually, in Grafton's words, "they implicated loved ones, friends and members of other Jewish communities". Thus did torture force innocent civilians to confess to fantastical crimes. Oxford historian Lyndal Roper found that the tortured eventually accepted the view that they were guilty.

Grafton's conclusion is unanswerable. Torture does not obtain truth. It will make most ordinary people say anything the torturer wants. Why, who knows if the men under the CIA's "waterboarding" did not confess that they could fly to meet the devil. And who knows if the CIA did not end up believing him.

CHAPTER 4

| What Should Be the
| U.S. Policy on Torture?

Chapter Preface

Torture is explicitly prohibited under international and U.S. law. The official U.S. policy on torture is to uphold its commitments to international prohibitions against torture contained in the 1948 Universal Declaration of Human Rights; the International Covenant on Civil and Political Rights; the Convention Against Torture or Other Cruel, Inhuman or Degrading Treatment or Punishment; and the Geneva Conventions, a series of international treaties governing the treatment of prisoners of war. As the assistant U.S. secretary of state for democracy, human rights, and labor reported to the United Nations in 1999:

> [Torture] is categorically denounced as a matter of [U.S.] policy and as a tool of state authority. In every instance, torture is a criminal offense. No official of the government—federal, state, or local, civilian or military—is authorized to commit or to instruct anyone else to commit torture. Nor may any official condone or tolerate torture in any form. No exceptional circumstances may be invoked as a justification for torture.

Most experts also believe that the U.S. Constitution prohibits torture. Various amendments in the Bill of Rights protect against torture: the Fourth Amendment's right to be free of unreasonable search or seizure (which encompasses the right not to be abused by the police); the Fifth Amendment's right against self-incrimination (which encompasses the right to remain silent during interrogations); the Fifth and the Fourteenth Amendments' guarantees of due process (ensuring fundamental fairness in the criminal justice system); and the Eighth Amendment's right to be free of cruel or unusual punishment.

Following the terrorist attacks of September 11, 2001, however, the George W. Bush administration appeared to change U.S. policy by carving out various exceptions to the U.S. torture ban. One change was the administration's declaration that terrorist suspects detained by U.S. forces in the war on terror were not prisoners of war subject to the Geneva Conventions but rather "enemy combatants" who were not entitled to either international or constitutional rights. At first, this label was applied only to foreigners detained in Afghanistan and Iraq, most of whom were then held at U.S. detention facilities in Abu Ghraib prison in Iraq and Guantánamo Bay, Cuba. But in 2002, the U.S. Department of Justice revealed that two citizens also had been classified as enemy combatants—one person being held at U.S. facilities in Guantánamo Bay, Cuba (Yaser Hamdi), and an American arrested in Chicago (Jose Padilla). Instead of providing enemy combatants access to U.S. courts, the administration set up an alternative system of military commissions that provided far fewer rights to the detainees. Yet another change in policy involved the administration's insistence that certain harsh, or what the administration called "enhanced," interrogation techniques used against enemy combatants in U.S. custody did not rise to the level of torture.

Although the administration argued that enemy combatants should have no access to U.S. courts, the U.S. Supreme Court agreed to hear several cases involving enemy combatants. In the first case decided in 2002, the Court sided with the president, ruling in *Rumsfeld v. Padilla* that American citizens could be designated and held as "enemy combatants."

Two years later, the Court began to challenge some of the administration's decisions in the war on terror. In 2004, in *Rumsfeld v. Hamdi*, the Court ruled that U.S.-born citizen and enemy combatant Yaser Hamdi could not be detained without giving him a way to challenge the government's evidence. In a second case also decided in 2004, *Rasul v. Bush*, the Court ruled that federal courts do have jurisdiction over enemy combatants held at Guantánamo Bay even though it is not on

U.S. soil. And in June 2006, the Court held in *Hamdan v. Rumsfeld* that the administration's military commissions were illegal because they violated the Geneva Conventions. The most recent Supreme Court action was in 2008, when the Court ruled in two cases, *Boumediene v. Bush* and *Al Odah v. United States,* that neither the president nor the Congress has the authority to strip detainees held in Guantánamo Bay of the right to habeas corpus—that is, the right to challenge their imprisonment.

Amnesty International, an anti-torture advocacy group, claims that the Bush administration is moving toward holding show trials by military commission at which the government plans to pursue the death penalty.

The Supreme Court, however, declined to hear a case explicitly involving torture brought by Khalid El-Masri, a German citizen who claimed that he was mistreated by U.S. interrogators in a prison in Afghanistan in violation of his rights under the U.S. Constitution and international law. The Court's decision not to review *El-Masri v. United States* meant that the lower court's decision in favor of the administration stands. The lower court rejected El-Masri's claim, holding that the case posed an unreasonable risk that privileged state secrets would be disclosed.

Additionally, following the Supreme Court's 2006 decision in *Hamdan v. Rumsfeld,* the president convinced Congress to pass legislation called the Military Commissions Act, restoring the government's right to try enemy combatants by military commission. Critics complained that the law basically strips detainees of their habeas corpus rights, sanctions endless detention without trial, and allows the use of tortured testimony before Guantánamo's military commissions. Most significantly, critics said, the law allows U.S. interrogators to use psychological torture by embracing a narrow definition of "severe mental pain." Many experts believe this definition allows the continued use of enhanced interrogation techniques, such as intensive interrogation; shackling; forcing detainees to hold themselves in stressful positions; sleep deprivation; isolation; extremes of heat and cold, light and dark, and noise and silence; sexual humiliation; use of dogs and other exploitations of detainees' fears and phobias; and waterboarding. In 2008, the concerns about enhanced interrogation techniques seemed to be confirmed when director of the Central Intelligence Agency (CIA) General Michael Hayden testified that waterboarding, or simulated drowning, was indeed one of the practices used by the CIA.

Responding to the growing concerns about torture, the Congress passed the 2008 Intelligence Authorization Act, adding a provision to ban enhanced interrogation practices and require the humane treatment of all prisoners. However, in March 2008, the president vetoed this bill, insisting that U.S. interrogators needed these tools to fight the war on terror. Amnesty International, an anti-torture advocacy group, claims that the Bush administration is moving toward holding show trials by military commission at which the government plans to pursue the death penalty.

The issue of the U.S. policy on torture and treatment of persons detained as part of the war on terror likely will be a question for President Barack Obama. The following viewpoints present some of the differing policy proposals on this important issue.

Stress Techniques Must Be Authorized in the War on Terror

Heather Mac Donald

Heather Mac Donald is a fellow at the Manhattan Institute, a public policy research organization, and a contributing editor to the Institute's urban-policy magazine, City Journal.

It didn't take long for interrogators in the war on terror to realize that their part was not going according to script. Pentagon doctrine, honed over decades of cold-war planning, held that 95 percent of prisoners would break upon straightforward questioning. Interrogators in Afghanistan, and later in Cuba and Iraq, found just the opposite: virtually none of the terror detainees was giving up information—not in response to direct questioning, and not in response to army-approved psychological gambits for prisoners of war.

The Damage Done by the Abu Ghraib Photos

Debate erupted in detention centers across the globe about how to get detainees to talk. Were "stress techniques"—such as isolation or sleep deprivation to decrease a detainee's resistance to questioning—acceptable? Before the discussion concluded, however, the photos of prisoner abuse in Iraq's Abu Ghraib prison appeared. Though they showed the sadism of a prison out of control, they showed nothing about interrogation.

Nevertheless, [George W.] Bush-administration critics seized on the scandal as proof that prisoner "torture" had become routine. A master narrative—call it the "torture narra-

Heather Mac Donald, "How to Interrogate Terrorists," *City Journal*, Winter 2005. www.city-journal.org. Reproduced by permission.

tive"—sprang up: the government's 2002 decision to deny Geneva-convention [international treaties governing the treatment of prisoners of war] status to al-Qaida fighters, it held, "led directly to the abuse of detainees in Afghanistan and Iraq," to quote the *Washington Post*. In particular, torturous interrogation methods, developed at Guantánamo Bay and Afghanistan in illegal disregard of Geneva protections, migrated to Abu Ghraib and were manifest in the abuse photos.

The Islamist enemy is unlike any the military has encountered in the past.

This story's success depends on the reader's remaining ignorant of the actual interrogation techniques promulgated in the war on terror. Not only were they light years from real torture and hedged around with bureaucratic safeguards, but they had nothing to do with the Abu Ghraib anarchy. Moreover, the decision on the Geneva conventions was irrelevant to interrogation practices in Iraq.

No matter. The Pentagon's reaction to the scandal was swift and sweeping. It stripped interrogators not just of stress options but of traditional techniques long regarded as uncontroversial as well. Red tape now entangles the interrogation process, and detainees know that their adversaries' hands are tied.

Dealing with the Islamist Enemy

The need for rethinking interrogation doctrine in the war on terror will not go away, however. The Islamist enemy is unlike any the military has encountered in the past. If current wisdom on the rules of war prohibits making any distinction between a terrorist and a lawful combatant, then that orthodoxy needs to change.

The interrogation debate first broke out on the frigid plains of Afghanistan. Marines and other special forces would dump planeloads of al-Qaida and Taliban prisoners into a ramshackle detention facility outside the Kandahar [a city in Afghanistan] airport; waiting interrogators were then supposed to extract information to be fed immediately back into the battlefield—whether a particular mountain pass was booby-trapped, say, or where an arms cache lay. That "tactical" debriefing accomplished, the Kandahar interrogation crew would determine which prisoners were significant enough to be shipped on to the Guantánamo naval base in Cuba for high-level interrogation.

Some of the al-Qaida fighters had received resistance training, which taught that Americans were strictly limited in how they could question prisoners.

Army doctrine gives interrogators 16 "approaches" to induce prisoners of war to divulge critical information. Sporting names like "Pride and Ego Down" and "Fear Up Harsh," these approaches aim to exploit a detainee's self-love, allegiance to or resentment of comrades, or sense of futility. Applied in the right combination, they will work on nearly everyone, the intelligence soldiers had learned in their training.

But the Kandahar prisoners were not playing by the army rule book. They divulged nothing. "Prisoners overcame the [traditional] model almost effortlessly," writes Chris Mackey in *The Interrogators*, his gripping account of his interrogation service in Afghanistan. The prisoners confounded their captors "not with clever cover stories but with simple refusal to cooperate. They offered lame stories, pretended not to remember even the most basic of details, and then waited for consequences that never really came."

Some of the al-Qaida fighters had received resistance training, which taught that Americans were strictly limited in how they could question prisoners. Failure to cooperate, the al-

Qaida manuals revealed, carried no penalties and certainly no risk of torture—a sign, gloated the manuals, of American weakness.

"Love of family" often had little purchase among the terrorists, however—as did love of life.

Even if a prisoner had not previously studied American detention policies before arriving at Kandahar, he soon figured them out. "It became very clear very early on to the detainees that the Americans were just going to have them sit there," recalls interrogator Joe Martin (a pseudonym). "They realized: 'The Americans will give us our Holy Book, they'll draw lines on the floor showing us where to pray, we'll get three meals a day with fresh fruit, do Jazzercise with the guards, . . . we can wait them out.'"

Even more challenging was that these detainees bore little resemblance to traditional prisoners of war. The army's interrogation manual presumed adversaries who were essentially the mirror image of their captors, motivated by emotions that all soldiers share. A senior intelligence official who debriefed prisoners in the 1989 U.S. operation in Panama contrasts the battlefield then and now: "There were no martyrs down there, believe me," he chuckles. "The Panamanian forces were more understandable people for us. Interrogation was pretty straightforward: 'Love of Family' [an army-manual approach, promising, say, contact with wife or children in exchange for cooperation] or, 'Here's how you get out of here as fast as you can.'"

"Love of family" often had little purchase among the terrorists, however—as did love of life. "The jihadists would tell you, 'I've divorced this life, I don't care about my family,'" recalls an interrogator at Guantánamo. "You couldn't shame them." The fierce hatred that the captives bore their captors heightened their resistance. The U.S. ambassador to Pakistan reported in January 2002 that prisoners in Kandahar would "shout epithets at their captors, including threats against the female relatives of the soldiers guarding them, knee marines in the groin, and say that they will escape and kill 'more Americans and Jews.'" Such animosity continued in Guantánamo.

Many of the [U.S.] interrogators argued for a calibrated use of "stress techniques"—long interrogations that would cut into the detainees' sleep schedules, for example.

Interrogators' Call for Stress Techniques

Battlefield commanders in Afghanistan and intelligence officials in Washington kept pressing for information, however. The frustrated interrogators constantly discussed how to get it. The best hope, they agreed, was to re-create the "shock of capture"—that vulnerable mental state when a prisoner is most frightened, most uncertain, and most likely to respond to questioning. Uncertainty is an interrogator's most powerful ally; exploited wisely, it can lead the detainee to believe that the interrogator is in total control and holds the key to his future. The Kandahar detainees, however, learned almost immediately what their future held, no matter how egregious their behavior: nothing untoward.

Many of the interrogators argued for a calibrated use of "stress techniques"—long interrogations that would cut into the detainees' sleep schedules, for example, or making a prisoner kneel or stand, or aggressive questioning that would put a detainee on edge.

Joe Martin—a crack interrogator who discovered that a top al-Qaida leader, whom Pakistan claimed to have in custody, was still at large and directing the Afghani resistance—explains the psychological effect of stress: "Let's say a detainee comes into the interrogation booth and he's had resistance training. He knows that I'm completely handcuffed and that I can't do anything to him. If I throw a temper tantrum, lift him onto his knees, and walk out, you can feel his uncertainty level rise dramatically. He's been told: 'They won't physically touch you,' and now you have. The point is not to beat him up but to introduce the reality into his mind that he doesn't know where your limit is." Grabbing someone by the top of the collar has had a more profound effect on the outcome of questioning than any actual torture could have, Martin maintains. "The guy knows: You just broke your own rules, and that's scary. He might demand to talk to my supervisor. I'll respond: 'There are no supervisors here,' and give him a maniacal smile."

President Bush had declared in February 2002 that al-Qaida members fell wholly outside the [Geneva] conventions.

Complying with the Geneva Conventions

The question was: Was such treatment consistent with the Geneva conventions?

President [George W.] Bush had declared in February 2002 that al-Qaida members fell wholly outside the conventions and that Taliban prisoners would not receive prisoner-of-war status—without which they, too, would not be covered by the Geneva rules. Bush ordered, however, that detainees be treated humanely and in accordance with Geneva principles, to the extent consistent with military necessity. This second pronouncement sank in: all of the war on terror's detention facilities chose to operate under Geneva rules. Contrary to the fulminations of rights advocates and the press, writes Chris Mackey, "Every signal we interrogators got from above from the colonels at [the Combined Forces Land Component Command] in Kuwait to the officers at Central Command back in

Tampa—had been . . . to observe the Conventions, respect prisoners' rights, and never cut corners."

What emerged was a hybrid and fluid set of detention practices. As interrogators tried to overcome the prisoners' resistance, their reference point remained Geneva and other humanitarian treaties. But the interrogators pushed into the outer limits of what they thought the law allowed, undoubtedly recognizing that the prisoners in their control violated everything the pacts stood for.

Did the stress techniques work? Yes.

The Geneva conventions embody the idea that even in as brutal an activity as war, civilized nations could obey humanitarian rules: no attacking civilians and no retaliation against enemy soldiers once they fall into your hands. Destruction would be limited as much as possible to professional soldiers on the battlefield. That rule required, unconditionally, that soldiers distinguish themselves from civilians by wearing uniforms and carrying arms openly.

Obedience to Geneva rules rests on another bedrock moral principle: reciprocity. Nations will treat an enemy's soldiers humanely because they want and expect their adversaries to do the same. Terrorists flout every civilized norm animating the conventions. Their whole purpose is to kill noncombatants, to blend into civilian populations, and to conceal their weapons. They pay no heed whatever to the golden rule; anyone who falls into their hands will most certainly not enjoy commissary privileges and wages, per the Geneva mandates. He—or she—may even lose his head.

Even so, terror interrogators tried to follow the spirit of the Geneva code for conventional, uniformed prisoners of war. That meant, as the code puts it, that the detainees could not be tortured or subjected to "any form of coercion" in order to secure information. They were to be "humanely" treated, protected against "unpleasant or disadvantageous treatment of any kind," and were entitled to "respect for their persons and their honour."

The Kandahar interrogators reached the following rule of thumb, reports Mackey: if a type of behavior toward a prisoner was no worse than the way the army treated its own members, it could not be considered torture or a violation of the conventions. Thus, questioning a detainee past his bedtime was lawful as long as his interrogator stayed up with him. If the interrogator was missing exactly the same amount of sleep as the detainee—and no tag-teaming of interrogators would be allowed, the soldiers decided—then sleep deprivation could not be deemed torture. In fact, interrogators were routinely sleep-deprived, catnapping maybe one or two hours a night, even as the detainees were getting long beauty sleeps. Likewise, if a boot-camp drill sergeant can make a recruit kneel with his arms stretched out in front without violating the Convention Against Torture, an interrogator can use that tool against a recalcitrant terror suspect.

Did the stress techniques work? Yes. "The harsher methods we used ... the better information we got and the sooner we got it," writes Mackey, who emphasizes that the methods never contravened the conventions or crossed over into torture. . . .

The End of Stress Techniques

That experiment [with stress techniques] is over. Reeling under the PR [public relations] disaster of Abu Ghraib, the Pentagon shut down every stress technique but one—isolation—and that can be used only after extensive review. An interrogator who so much as requests permission to question a detainee into the night could be putting his career in jeopardy. Even the traditional army psychological approaches have fallen under a deep cloud of suspicion: deflating a detainee's ego, aggressive but non-physical histrionics, and good cop–bad cop have been banished along with sleep deprivation.

Timidity among officers prevents the energetic application of those techniques that remain. Interrogation plans have to be triple-checked all the way up through the Pentagon by officers who have never conducted an interrogation in their lives.

In losing these techniques, interrogators have lost the ability to create the uncertainty vital to getting terrorist information. Since the Abu Ghraib scandal broke, the military has made public nearly every record of its internal interrogation debates, providing al-Qaida analysts with an encyclopedia of U.S. methods and constraints. Those constraints make perfectly clear that the interrogator is not in control. "In reassuring the world about our limits, we have destroyed our biggest asset: detainee doubt," a senior Pentagon intelligence official laments.

Soldiers on the ground are noticing the consequences. "The Iraqis already know the game. They know how to play us," a marine chief warrant officer told the *Wall Street Journal* in August. "Unless you catch the Iraqis in the act, it is very hard to pin anything on anyone. . . . We can't even use basic police interrogation tactics."

And now the rights advocates, energized by the Abu Ghraib debacle, are making one final push to halt interrogation altogether. In the *New York Times*'s words, the International Committee of the Red Cross (ICRC) is now condemning the thoroughly emasculated interrogation process at Guantánamo Bay as a "system devised to break the will of the prisoners [and] make them wholly dependent on their interrogators." In other words, the ICRC opposes traditional interrogation itself, since *all* interrogation is designed to "break the will of prisoners" and make them feel "dependent on their interrogators." But according to an ICRC report leaked to the *Times*, "the construction of such a system, whose stated purpose is the production of intelligence, cannot be considered other than an intentional system of cruel, unusual and degrading treatment and a form of torture."

But contrary to the fantasies of the international-law and human rights lobbies, a world in which all interrogation is illegal and rights are indiscriminately doled out is not a safer or more just world. Were the United States to announce that terrorists would be protected under the Geneva conventions, it would destroy any incentive our ruthless enemies have to comply with the laws of war. The *Washington Post* and the *New York Times* understood that truth in 1987, when they supported President Ronald Reagan's rejection of an amendment to the Geneva conventions that would have granted lawful-combatant status to terrorists. Today, however, those same opinion makers have done an about-face, though the most striking feature of their denunciations of the Bush administration's Geneva decisions is their failure to offer any explanation for how al-Qaida could possibly be covered under the plain meaning of the text.

Deciding Rules for the Future

The Pentagon is revising the rules for interrogation. If we hope to succeed in the war on terror, the final product *must* allow interrogators to use stress techniques against unlawful combatants. Chris Mackey testifies to how "ineffective schoolhouse methods were in getting prisoners to talk." He warns that his team "failed to break prisoners who I have no doubt knew of terrorist plots or at least terrorist cells that may one day do us harm. Perhaps they would have talked if faced with harsher methods."

The stress techniques that the military has used to date are not torture; the advocates can only be posturing in calling them such. On its website, Human Rights Watch [an anti-torture advocacy group] lists the effects of real torture: "from pain and swelling to broken bones, irreparable neurological damage, and chronic painful musculoskeletal problems . . . [to] long-term depression, post-traumatic stress disorder, marked sleep disturbances and alterations in self-perceptions, not to mention feelings of powerlessness, of fear, guilt and shame." Though none of the techniques that Pentagon interrogators have employed against al-Qaida comes anywhere close to risking such effects, Human Rights Watch nevertheless follows up its list with an accusation of torture against the Bush administration.

The pressure on the Pentagon to outlaw stress techniques won't abate, as the American Civil Liberties Union [a civil rights organization] continues to release formerly classified government documents obtained in a Freedom of Information Act lawsuit concerning detention and interrogation. As of late December, the memos have merely confirmed that the FBI [Federal Bureau of Investigation] opposes stress methods, though the press breathlessly portrays them as confirming "torture."

Human Rights Watch, the ICRC, Amnesty International, and the other self-professed guardians of humanitarianism need to come back to earth—to the real world in which torture means what the Nazis and the Japanese did in their concentration and POW camps in World War II; the world in which evil regimes, like those we fought in Afghanistan and Iraq, don't follow the Miranda rules or the Convention Against Torture but instead gas children, bury people alive, set wild animals on soccer players who lose, and hang adulterous women by truckloads before stadiums full of spectators; the world in which barbarous death cults behead female aid workers, bomb crowded railway stations, and fly planes filled with hundreds of innocent passengers into buildings filled with thousands of innocent and unsuspecting civilians. By definition, our terrorist enemies and their state supporters have declared themselves enemies of the civilized order and its humanitarian rules. In fighting them, we must of course hold ourselves to our own high moral standards without, however, succumbing to the utopian illusion that we can prevail while immaculately observing every precept of the Sermon on the Mount. It is the necessity of this fallen world that we must oppose evil with force; and we must use all the lawful means necessary to ensure that good, rather than evil, triumphs.

The United States Should Stop All Forms of Torture

Washington Monthly

Washington Monthly *is a magazine that covers U.S. politics, government, and culture.*

In most issues of the *Washington Monthly*, we favor articles that we hope will launch a debate. In this issue we seek to end one. The unifying message . . . is, simply, *Stop*. In the wake of September 11 [the 2001 terrorist attacks on the United States], the United States became a nation that practiced torture. Astonishingly—despite the repudiation of torture by experts and the revelations of Guantanamo and Abu Ghraib [U.S. detention facilities in Cuba and Iraq]—we remain one. As we go to press [early 2008], President George W. Bush stands poised to veto a measure that would end all use of torture by the United States. His move, we suspect, will provoke only limited outcry. What once was shocking is now ordinary.

U.S. Interrogation Techniques

On paper, the list of practices declared legal by the Department of Justice for use on detainees in Guantanamo Bay and other locations has a somewhat bloodless quality—sleep deprivation, stress positions, forced standing, sensory deprivation, nudity, extremes of heat or cold. But such bland terms mask great suffering. Sleep deprivation eventually leads to hallucinations and psychosis. (Menachem Begin, former prime minister of Israel, experienced sleep deprivation at the hands of the KGB [Russian intelligence agents] and would later assert that "anyone who has experienced this desire [to sleep] knows that not even hunger and thirst are comparable with it.") Stress

Washington Monthly, "No More: No Torture, No Exceptions," January/February/March 2008. www.washingtonmonthly.com. Copyright © 2008 *Washington Monthly*. Reproduced by permission.

positions entail ordeals such as being shackled by the wrists, suspended from the ceiling, with arms spread out and feet barely touching the ground. Forced standing, a technique often used in North Korean prisons, involves remaining erect and completely still, producing an excruciating combination of physical and psychological pain, as ankles swell, blisters erupt on the skin, and, in time, kidneys break down. Sensory deprivation—being deprived of sight, sound, and touch—can produce psychotic symptoms in as little as twenty-four hours. The agony of severe and prolonged exposure to temperature extremes and the humiliation of forced nudity speak for themselves.

Then there is waterboarding, a form of mock execution by drowning, a technique that has been used in so-called "black sites." In addition to the physical pain and terror it induces, long-term psychological effects also haunt patients—panic attacks, depression, and symptoms of post-traumatic-stress disorder. It has long been prosecuted as a crime of war. In our view, it still should be.

Years from now, what will shame us most is that our country abandoned a bedrock principle of civilized nations: that torture is without exception wrong.

The Future

Ideally, the election in November [2008] would put an end to this debate, but we fear it won't. [Sen.] John McCain, who for so long was one of the leading Republican opponents of the White House's policy on torture, voted in February against making the CIA [Central Intelligence Agency] subject to the ban on "enhanced interrogation." As for [Sen.] Hillary Clinton and [Sen.] Barack Obama, while both have come out strongly against torture, they seldom discuss the subject on the campaign trail. We fear that even a Democratic president might, under pressure from elements of the national security bureaucracy, carve out loopholes, possibly in secret, condoning some forms of torture.

Over the past decade, voters have had many legitimate worries: stagnant wages, corruption in Washington, terrorism, and a botched war in Iraq. But we believe that when Americans look back years from now, what will shame us most is that our country abandoned a bedrock principle of civilized nations: that torture is without exception wrong. . . .

It was a profound moral and strategic mistake for the United States to abandon long-standing policies of humane treatment of enemy captives. We should return to the rule of law and cease all forms of torture, with no exceptions for any agency. And we should expect our presidential nominees to commit to this idea.

Torture Should Be Made Legal in Extreme Situations

Alan M. Dershowitz

Alan M. Dershowitz is a lawyer, author, political commentator, and professor of law at Harvard Law School.

Several years ago, I provoked a storm of controversy by advocating "torture warrants" as a way of creating accountability for the use of torture in terrorism cases. I argued that if we were ever to encounter a "ticking bomb" situation in which the authorities believed that an impending terror attack could be prevented only by torturing a captured terrorist into revealing the location of the bomb, the authorities would, in fact, employ such a tactic.

Former President Clinton's Proposal

Although I personally oppose the use of torture, I recognize the reality that some forms of torture have been, are being and will continue to be used by democracies in extreme situations, regardless of what we say or what the law provides. In an effort to limit the use of torture to genuinely extreme "ticking bomb" situations, rather than allowing it to become as routine as it obviously became at Abu Ghraib [a U.S. detention facility in Iraq], I proposed that the president or a federal judge would have to take personal responsibility for ordering its use in extraordinary situations.

For suggesting this approach to the terrible choice of evils between torture and terrorism, I was condemned as a moral monster, labeled an advocate of torture and called a Torquemada.

Now I see that former President [Bill] Clinton has offered a similar proposal. In a recent interview on National Public

Alan M. Dershowitz, "Warming Up to Torture?" *Los Angeles Times*, October 17, 2006. www.latimes.com. Reproduced by permission.

Radio, Clinton was asked, as someone "who's been there," whether the president needs "the option of authorizing torture in an extreme case."

This is what he said in response: "Look, if the president needed an option, there's all sorts of things they can do. Let's take the best case, OK. You picked up someone you know is the No. 2 aide to Osama bin Laden. And you know they have an operation planned for the United States or some European capital in the next . . . three days. And you know this guy knows it. Right, that's the clearest example. And you think you can only get it out of this guy by shooting him full of some drugs or water-boarding him or otherwise working him over. If they really believed that that scenario is likely to occur, let them come forward with an alternate proposal.

[Former president Bill] Clinton . . . would, in extreme cases, authorize the granting of a [torture] warrant "post facto" by a specialized court.

"We have a system of laws here where nobody should be above the law, and you don't need blanket advance approval for blanket torture. They can draw a statute much more narrowly, which would permit the president to make a finding in a case like I just outlined, and then that finding could be submitted even if after the fact to the Foreign Intelligence Surveillance Court."

Clinton was then asked whether he was saying there "would be more responsibility afterward for what was done." He replied: "Yeah, well, the president could take personal responsibility for it. But you do it on a case-by-case basis, and there'd be some review of it." Clinton quickly added that he doesn't know whether this ticking bomb scenario "is likely or not," but he did know that "we have erred in who was a real suspect or not."

Clinton summarized his views in the following terms: "If they really believe the time comes when the only way they can get a reliable piece of information is to beat it out of someone or put a drug in their body to talk it out of 'em, then they can present it to the Foreign Intelligence Court, or some other court, just under the same circumstances we do with wiretaps. Post facto. . . .

"But I think if you go around passing laws that legitimize a violation of the Geneva Convention [international treaties governing the treatment of prisoners of war] and institutionalize what happened at Abu Ghraib or Guantanamo [a U.S. detention facility in Cuba], we're gonna be in real trouble."

Let's not stop thinking and talking about whether the evil of torture is ever a necessary evil.

"Post Facto" Warrants

It is surprising that this interview with the former president has received so little attention from those who were so quick to jump all over me. Clinton goes even further than I did. He would, in extreme cases, authorize the granting of a warrant "post facto" by a specialized court, as is now the case with national security wiretaps. What I proposed is that the warrant authorization be issued *before* the use of extreme measures is permitted. A preliminary warrant could be issued in a manner of minutes, to be followed up by a more thorough, after-the-fact evaluation and review.

I offered my controversial proposal as a way to stimulate debate about a difficult choice of evils. I hope that the silence following the Clinton interview does not mean the debate has ended. The problem persists. Torture will continue. Let's not stop thinking and talking about whether the evil of torture is ever a necessary evil.

Torture Should Not Be Legally Sanctioned

Jack Rabbit

Jack Rabbit is a poet, essayist, and blogger from Sacramento, California.

Alan Dershowitz, the renowned legal scholar and civil libertarian, has stirred up a small hornet's nest since the September 11 [2001] attacks by talking openly about the possibilities of sanctioning torture in America. Dershowitz feels it is incumbent on him to lead a discussion on a choice he feels is unpleasant but necessary.

Laws Against Torture

Torture is regarded by progressive civil libertarians as an abomination that every civilized nation should outlaw. Modern international humanitarian law categorically prohibits its use. The Rome Statute [a treaty that established the International Criminal Court] classifies torture as a crime against humanity, the Third Geneva Convention (1949) prohibits its use against prisoners of war and the Fourth Geneva Convention (1949) prohibits it against civilians in situations of armed conflict. The United Nations Declaration of Human Rights (1948) states unequivocally, "No one shall be subjected to torture or to cruel, inhuman or degrading treatment or punishment." Gloss is put on these declarations concerning torture by the Convention Against Torture and Other Cruel, Inhuman or Degrading Treatment or Punishment (1984), to which the United States is a party.

The Convention defines *torture*:

> For the purposes of this Convention, the term "torture" means any act by which severe pain or suffering, whether

physical or mental, is intentionally inflicted on a person for such purposes as obtaining from him or a third person information or a confession, punishing him for an act he or a third person has committed or is suspected of having committed, or intimidating or coercing him or a third person, or for any reason based on discrimination of any kind, when such pain or suffering is inflicted by or at the instigation of or with the consent or acquiescence of a public official or other person acting in an official capacity. It does not include pain or suffering arising only from, inherent in or incidental to lawful sanctions.

Dershowitz's Argument

Dershowitz is regarded by many as a progressive civil libertarian. That he should part company with others on a matter that many feel defines progressivism has outraged more than a few. However, when one such as Dershowitz suggests that we cast aside much of what we hold dear, perhaps we should give him a hearing.

Dershowitz' argument can be easily misconstrued if it is not read. An opinion piece written by Dershowitz for the *Los Angeles Times* (November 8, 2001) outlines his position; a reader can get a better idea of Dershowitz' thesis by reading Chapter 4 of his ... [2002] book, *Why Terrorism Works: Understanding the Threat, Responding to the Challenge*. It should be understood from the start that Dershowitz is suggesting only "nonlethal" forms of torture aimed at extracting information in national security cases, such as those involving a planned terrorist attack, and other cases where the potential for loss of human life would be catastrophic. Moreover, Dershowitz is very much aware of the constitutional issues surrounding the use of torture; Dershowitz is quite aware that no information extracted under torture could be used against the informant in any criminal proceedings. Dershowitz deserves to be lauded for having his priorities straight enough to opt, when presented with an exclusive choice of one or the other, for preventing the execution of the crime and saving lives over prosecuting and punishing the criminal.

Of course, that choice is one given in a hypothetical situation. Law professors often present hypothetical situations as teaching aides. They provide neat, clear cases where the student has no trouble recognizing how the legal principle is applied to given facts. To advance his ideas about the proper use of torture, Dershowitz uses the ticking bomb scenario. Mr. Dershowitz explains the case by quoting another scholar, Michael Walzer:

> [A] decent leader of a nation plagued with terrorism is asked "to authorize the torture of a captured rebel leader who knows or probably knows the location of a number of bombs hidden in apartment buildings across the city, set to go off within the next twenty-four hours. He orders the man tortured, convinced he must do so for the sake of the people who might otherwise die in the explosions—even though he believes torture is wrong, indeed abominable, not just sometimes, but always."

The ticking bomb case fails to show how it is necessary to torture the suspect in order to save lives.

Dershowitz argues that the hypothetical leader acted justly in this hypothetical situation. Indeed, the facts given as they are might make a good case for torture. Many of us who regard torture as a clear crime against humanity are grasping to hold our own position in light of this case.

Since Dershowitz is not unaware of the constitutional problems inherent with this position, he offers the legal remedy of controls and supervision over torture. Rather than prohibit torture, as would a progressive civil libertarian, he would legally sanction torture and allow judges to issue a warrant for its use.

On the one hand, progressive civil libertarians seem stuck. Dershowitz' case for legally supervised, nonlethal torture appears to be rooted in good logic in which the conclusions fall neatly from their premises. However, the conclusion reached is so odious that one still strives to reject it. To progressive civil libertarians attempting to hold the line in the context of a national debate in which [President George W.] Bush and [former Attorney General John] Ashcroft ... [sought] broad powers to abrogate civil liberties, even to strip Americans of their citizenship, and mock[ed] the Third Geneva Convention daily in Guantanamo [a U.S. detention facility in Cuba], Dershowitz appears to have gone over to the dark side.

On the other hand, Dershowitz' defenders, many of whom are less committed to progressive principles and the rule of law than was Dershowitz in the past, claim that the post-September 11 world has changed everything and that pre-September 11 notions about civilized behavior regarding the treatment of at least a certain class of criminal suspects is just not practical.

The information gained from a torture victim must be regarded as unreliable.

Flaws in Dershowitz's Argument on the Ticking Bomb Scenario

However, progressive civil libertarians need not concede a single point to Dershowitz, let alone the supporters of Bush and Ashcroft. There are at least three problems with Dershowitz' case for torture, all of which are fatal.

One problem with Dershowitz' argument is that it is based on a hypothetical situation. Something so clear would seldom, if ever, exist in the real world. On close examination, the ticking bomb case is exposed as absurd and the problems of Dershowitz' case begins to disappear.

The ticking bomb scenario assumes a situation where the authorities know about a plotted crime, but still don't know enough to begin an effective investigation. Somehow, we are supposed to believe that there might be a situation where authorities have certain knowledge of a terrorist's guilt without knowing exactly of what he's guilty. In this case, the authorities know *who* with certainty (the terrorist leader they have in custody), they know *what* (a series of bombs set to go off around the city), they know *when* (within the next twenty-four hours), but they don't know exactly *where*. Does it seem realistic that they would know who, what and when, but not where? Wouldn't the same source of the information about the who, what and when not also know at least some specific locations of the bombs and some other possible ones? It seems unlikely that one would have information in such detail without knowing more than this scenario allows.

Even in the scenario as given, we are told that the bombs are planted in some undisclosed apartment buildings throughout the city. With so little time, the authorities' efforts might be better spent evacuating any potential target in order to save lives. Torturing the suspect won't help get people out of apartment buildings.

Thus, the ticking bomb case fails to show how it is necessary to torture the suspect in order to save lives.

Dershowitz also brings up the matter of Zacarias Moussaoui, who is currently in custody and awaiting trial for his part in the September 11 attacks. [Moussaoui was convicted in 2006 and is serving a life sentence.] Dershowitz presents his argument in this case as follows:

> The government decided not to seek a warrant to search his computer. Now imagine that they had, and discovered he was part of a plan to destroy large occupied buildings, but without any further details. They interrogated him, gave him immunity from prosecution, and offered him large cash rewards and a new identity. They threatened him, tried to

trick him and tried every lawful technique available. He still refused. They even injected him with sodium pentothal and other truth serums, but to no avail. The attack now appeared to be *imminent,* but the FBI [Federal Bureau of Investigation] had no idea what the target was or what means would be used to attack it. We could not simply evacuate all buildings indefinitely. An FBI agent proposes use of nonlethal torture. . . .

[Alan] Dershowitz fails to provide any example where he can unequivocally say that the information gained through torture could not have been gained by some other means.

What Dershowitz has done is to take an actual case and embellish it into a hypothetical one. This new scenario has one virtue of citing a specific person widely believed to be involved in a specific catastrophe. Otherwise, it is every bit as hypothetical and just as absurd as the ticking bomb case. It even helps to illustrate what is wrong with the previous scenario. Again, we are asked to suppose that the authorities found the broad outlines of the plan on a suspect's computer, but nothing else that would be useful to them. They have no way of knowing who Moussaoui's contacts were (in spite of looking at his e-mail on the same computer and probably . . . also checking his telephone records as well) or knowing who he might have talked with (in spite of also knowing where he lived and probably contacting an employer). We are also supposed to believe they have no information other than he is involved in a plot to destroy buildings, except that they also know exactly when this event is to happen.

Is all this too hypothetical? Yes, it is.

Dershowitz' scenario with the Moussaoui case removes the level of urgency that is inherent in the ticking bomb case. The authorities could pursue other leads and possibly uncover the details of the plot before the catastrophe takes place. There is no need to waste time interrogating an uncooperative suspect, by either conventional or extraordinary means.

Unreliable Information

The second problem is that the information gained from a torture victim must be regarded as unreliable. The authorities may torture a suspect . . . and he may tell them anything to get them to stop. Since the situation is urgent, time is on the side of the terrorist. If he is determined to kill people, he could tell them anything or even nothing at all. The authorities would have to investigate what he says, since they can't assume it is true. Of course, investigating the suspect's statements takes time that the authorities don't have. Torturing the suspect where time is an urgent factor gains the authorities nothing.

Dershowitz asserts that there are instances where torture has provided accurate information that has prevented harm to civilians. However, that does not change the fact the information gained under torture would still need to be investigated in order to be verified. Normally, police won't take any voluntary statement made by a suspect at face value unless they already have something to corroborate it. Any statements made under the duress of torture should be greeted with even more scrutiny. Says Dershowitz:

> It is impossible to avoid the difficult moral dilemma of choosing among evils by denying the empirical reality that torture *sometimes* works, even if it does not always work. No technique of crime prevention always works.

In other words, Dershowitz is admitting that information gained from a torture victim is not reliable. This is true both in Dershowitz' ticking bomb case, where time is an urgent factor, and his hypothetical Moussaoui case, where it is not, at least until the very end.

After making the categorical statement, "the tragic reality is that torture sometimes works," Dershowitz fails to provide any example where he can unequivocally say that the information gained through torture could not have been gained by some other means. The case he cites in the most detail, one arising from the Philippines in 1995 where a plot to blow up eleven passenger jets over the Pacific Ocean was foiled, involved sufficient time for authorities to investigate the plot based on information received. Dershowitz does not elaborate on the facts of this case, which involve the torture of Hakim Abdul Marud. The fact is that Marud was arrested by the authorities following a fire that started in his apartment. The fire was started as a result of Marud mixing chemicals, which was suspicious activity in the first place. The authorities found the evidence of the bombing plot on Marud's laptop computer. Marud was tortured for 67 days. Clearly, time was not a matter of urgency, as it is in the ticking bomb scenario. As in Dershowitz' hypothetical case involving Moussaoui, the authorities in the Marud case began with time to pursue leads without resorting to extraordinary methods of interrogation. It is entirely possible that the authorities in this case, using more conventional methods of investigation consistent with modern standards of civilized behavior, would have prevented the catastrophe just the same. It is clear from the facts provided that they had enough evidence to hold Marud and commence an investigation. Any claim that torture was necessary to prevent a catastrophe in this case is not provable.

[Alan] Dershowitz revives an old and long discarded concept from English law, the torture warrant.

A Time-Consuming Process

The final problem with Dershowitz' argument is that it involves a time-consuming process where time is urgent. In his admirable attempt to balance the needs of modern society facing a threat from the likes of [al-Qaeda leader] Osama [bin

Laden] with the demands of rule of law in a democratic society, Dershowitz would not simply have the authorities torture information out of a suspect, but would require that the process be given legal sanction and supervision. Dershowitz revives an old and long discarded concept from English law, the torture warrant. Torture was used to get information from unwilling suspects and witnesses under British law prior to the late eighteenth century. However, as Dershowitz points out, the requirement to convict under English law a criminal defendant was at that time either the confession of the accused or the testimony of two eyewitnesses to the crime; a case built entirely on circumstantial evidence was insufficient. This no longer applies. Today, a case may be built entirely on circumstantial evidence; for example, one of the many murders of which Charlie Manson was convicted [in 1971], that of Shorty Shea, was a case where the victim's body was not found until many years after the trial.

[Alan] Dershowitz does not propose any specific legal standards for the issuing of a torture warrant.

However, Dershowitz does not seek to use torture to gain a conviction. He is seeking to gain information to prevent a greater catastrophe. Nevertheless, Dershowitz points out that under English law, the ability to authorize torture was tightly controlled by the Privy Council [a body of advisors to the British king] in order to prevent local authorities from abusing the rights of defendants. This is the model he would use to institute torture in modern society. Dershowitz believes that if his recommendations are followed, torture . . . would be used only in the most extraordinary cases. As Dershowitz says:

> I believe that most judges would require compelling evidence before they would authorize so extraordinary a departure from our constitutional norms, and law enforcement

officials would be reluctant to seek a warrant unless they had compelling evidence that the suspect had information needed to prevent an imminent terrorist attack.

Nevertheless, Dershowitz does not propose any specific legal standards for the issuing of a torture warrant. If we were to examine ... his hypothetical cases and see what they have in common, we might arrive at a set of standards that could possibly be used: the situation at hand is *potentially catastrophic* and the loss of great numbers of human lives is at stake; there is a *suspect whose culpability is certain to a high standard of proof*; and there is an element of urgency in that the attack is imminent and there is no time to effectively pursue other avenues of investigation.

In the ticking bomb case, this standard might be impractical. In that scenario, the authorities have only twenty-four hours to get accurate information about the location of a series of bombs and defuse them. In this twenty-four hour period, the authorities would have to first get a warrant from a judge who would demand before issuing the warrant that they first prove to him that there is an imminent threat of a catastrophic event, that the suspect they hold has information that would prevent the execution of the threat, and that there is no time to try anything else; then they would have to torture the suspect; and then, since information gained from a suspect under torture must be regarded as unreliable, verify any information he provided. Perhaps after all that is done, they will still have time to defuse the bombs. However, it might be more practical to evacuate any building that even is remotely suspected of being a target, the entire city if necessary. The use of torture with all its trappings in the ticking bomb scenario becomes a reductio ad absurdum. The time-consuming processes of obtaining a warrant, extracting information from the suspect through torture and verifying the information simply defeat the purpose of interrogating the suspect.

Dershowitz' hypothetical case involving Zacarais Moussaoui is a little more problematic, if only because it is a little more difficult to ascertain from the way Dershowitz lays it out exactly what the authorities could take to a judge. Here, too, torture is not contemplated unless the threat is imminent; therefore, we must apply all the problems that defeat the ticking bomb case to this one. In addition, unless the authorities have a better idea of what is being threatened than Dershowitz provides in the scenario, they couldn't possibly prove that there is an imminent threat. The judge may want to ask them why they are holding him in custody with no more evidence than Dershowitz indicates they have. Here again, it seems improbable that the authorities have only the faintest information of a plot with no other details. The FBI agents assigned to the case in this scenario have been foolishly wasting time interrogating Moussaoui when they could have been checking out his every move since arriving in the United States, as real FBI agents would likely do.

> *[Alan] Dershowitz has thus failed to prove anything practical is to be gained by allowing legally sanctioned torture in extraordinary circumstances.*

Finally, we have the actual case of Hakim Abdul Marud in the Philippines, where the use of torture may have prevented a terrorist attack; however, neither Dershowitz nor his readers can say with certainty that it did, since nothing suggests that any other investigative technique was applied. If the FBI had been holding Marud under these rules, rather than Filipino intelligence agents with no rules, Marud probably would not have been tortured. It is clear that when the Filipino agents began torturing Marud, there was no imminent threat; after all, no terrorist attack was executed during the 67 days they tortured him. This case can't be used to demonstrate the strength of Dershowitz' thesis.

Many Arguments Against Legally Sanctioned Torture

Dershowitz has thus failed to prove anything practical is to be gained by allowing legally sanctioned torture in extraordinary circumstances. Since the burden of proof is on him to demonstrate that there is any benefit to altering current international conventions against the use of torture, the categorical prohibition expressed by those conventions should thus be respected.

In addition, there are many pragmatic reasons to continue to oppose the introduction of legally sanctioned torture. Dershowitz' own arguments are laced with proposals for protections of the rights of a suspect who faces torture because Dershowitz, rightly, recognizes that the potential for government abuse is rampant should torture be allowed. Obviously, many states choose to disregard international conventions. Dershowitz even observes that only in a democracy committed to civil liberties can this kind of discussion take place; in such states as Egypt, Jordan, Burma and Zimbabwe, leaders are not responsible to popular will and act as they see fit, often with less concern about national security than the security of their own hold on power. These states are part of the overall problem in the world today, not a model for any solution.

In the post-September 11 world, . . . international humanitarian law has replaced America as the great progressive hope of humanity.

Besides traditionally tyrannical regimes, there is a deterioration of democratic values among the leaders of states that not long ago seemed on the path to becoming democratic and even in states long regarded as beacons of democracy. In Russia, for which so many held high hopes when the Soviet Union collapsed, Vladimir Putin . . . [ran] virtually unopposed for President. Using terrorist attacks from Chechnyan rebels as a pretext, Putin has contracted civil liberties in Russia. More recently, opposition presidential candidates have complained of intimidation. According to the *London Observer*, Putin is . . . [in 2004] poised to become "the most powerful Russian leader since Stalin." In the United States, George W. Bush's authority as President [in his first term] rests not on a clear electoral victory but on a narrow and dubiously reasoned [2000] Supreme Court decision. He has used his power to enrich his corporations at state expense. Like Putin, Bush has used the terrorist attacks against his nation as a pretext to erode civil liberties and, . . . Bush has told brazen lies to manipulate his country into a war of dubious necessity.

Leaders such as Putin and Bush should not be trusted with the ultimate authority to sanction torture any more than [Egyptian President] Hosni Mubarak or [Saudi Arabia's] King Fahd. Whether any leader, elected or otherwise, should be so trusted is doubtful.

In the post-September 11 world, in which Mr. Bush's leadership has eroded America's moral position as a beacon of human dignity, international humanitarian law has replaced America as the great progressive hope of humanity. While Bush unilaterally declares battlefield detainees to be illegal combatants without rights under the Geneva Conventions and hurls them into dog kennels at Guantanamo, while his Justice Department drafts legislation to give him the right to strip an American of his citizenship, and while he contracts out to nations known to scorn human rights standards for the purpose of torturing terror suspects, international humanitarian law upholds our hope by declaring categorically that no human being should be subjected to torture or to cruel, inhuman or degrading treatment or punishment. This is the ideal to which we should strive.

The United States Should Categorically Ban Torture but Consider Rare Exceptions

Albert Mohler

Albert Mohler is an evangelical leader and president of The Southern Baptist Theological Seminary. He also hosts a daily live nationwide radio program and writes commentary on moral, cultural, and theological issues.

Looking back at World War I, Winston Churchill was moved to write: "When all was over, torture and cannibalism were the only two expedients that the civilized, scientific, Christian states had been able to deny themselves: and these were of doubtful utility." The "Great War" was a laboratory for human killing, with the first widespread use of mechanized weapons of mass murder like the machine gun and the tank. Accompanying these weapons were inventions such as aerial bombardment and poison gas. Yet, the war saw neither side institutionalize the use of torture. In the end, that was about all Churchill could claim on behalf of military restraint.

The question of torture arises once again in the context of the War on Terror and has been brought to public controversy with the amendment to the current Defense Authorization Bill sponsored by Senator John McCain. The measure, which would render illegal all "cruel, inhuman, or degrading" treatments of prisoners under U.S. control, passed by a vote of 90–9 in the full Senate. President George W. Bush had threatened to veto the legislation, if it were to be passed by the House of Representatives. On December 15 [2005], the White House announced that it would back the McCain Amendment.

Nevertheless, public debate over the amendment—and the issues of coercion and torture—will not end with the conclusion of this political drama, nor should it. This is a vital issue of great moral consequence, and this debate should not be allowed to slip from public view. All citizens bear responsibility to be informed and engaged concerning this question.

Without doubt, the scandals associated with prisoner abuse at Abu Ghraib ... have caused considerable embarrassment to the United States.

This debate was advanced through the contribution of columnist Charles Krauthammer and his article, "The Truth About Torture," published in the December 5, 2005 issue of *The Weekly Standard*. Krauthammer, a morally serious man, presents a morally serious argument against the McCain amendment—going so far as to suggest that McCain's position is something less than intellectually honest.

Both men deserve careful attention. Sen. John McCain is a man whose courage was demonstrated through the awful experience of imprisonment and torture at the hands of the North Vietnamese regime. Torture and the treatment of prisoners of war is no hypothetical issue to this senator. At the same time, Charles Krauthammer also deserves a respectful hearing. His background in medicine and the law, coupled with his own public courage and service as a member of the President's Council on Bioethics, summons our attention.

Krauthammer argues that "there is no denying the monstrous evil that is any form of torture," nor "how corrupting it can be for the individuals and society that practice it." But, he also believes that there are exceptions to this rule, and that these exceptions demand the discipline of rules.

"The problem with the McCain amendment," he asserts, "is that once you have gone public with a blanket ban on all forms of coercion, it is going to be very difficult to publicly carve out exceptions." Krauthammer then faults the Bush administration for "having attempted such a codification with the kind of secrecy, lack of coherence, and lack of strict enforcement that led us to the McCain reaction."

Coercion is a normal device for obtaining information in many contexts, including routine police interrogations.

Without doubt, the scandals associated with prisoner abuse at Abu Ghraib and the advice offered in the memo prepared by John Loo of the Office of Legal Counsel in the Department of Justice have caused considerable embarrassment to the United States. Are we a people who would allow torture to be used as an instrument of state power? More to the point, has the War on Terror changed the rules?

Krauthammer argues that the rules have indeed changed. Captured terrorists, he argues, are not soldiers captured in a conflict of arms, but something more like dangerous criminals who break the laws of war by killing and abusing civilians "for a living." Therefore, they are entitled "to nothing" in terms of rights, having forfeited such claims by becoming terrorists. And yet, he does not actually believe that they are entitled to *nothing*, for he would not sanction any and all uses of coercion and torture, just those that fit his description of exceptional cases.

"Torture is not always impermissible," Krauthammer allows. "However rare these cases, there are circumstances in which, by rational moral calculus, torture not only would be permissible but would be required (to acquire life-saving information). And once you've established the principle, to paraphrase George Bernard Shaw, all that's left to haggle about is the price."

McCain agrees, to a point. After all, he also accepts that exceptions will, even *must* be made under exceedingly rare circumstances. The difference between these two proposals is a distinction worthy of our most serious moral scrutiny and review. In the end, I must side with McCain, but not without further moral clarifications.

Most morally sensitive persons would surely allow interrogators to yell at prisoners and to use . . . [other coercive techniques] for purposes of obtaining vital information.

McCain and Krauthammer are both talking about coercion and torture for the purpose of acquiring vital information that would conceivably save lives—and for no other purpose. But when they speak of coercion and torture, do they mean the same things? Coercion is a normal device for obtaining information in many contexts, including routine police interrogations. Of course, the coercive techniques of normative police policy in the U.S. do not include the use of physical torture. Yet, some international agencies and policy groups define virtually any high-pressure interrogation or psychological techniques as torture. I agree with Jean Bethke Elshtain when she suggests that those who advocate such expansive claims make "mincement" of vital terms and categories. She rightly suggests that sleep deprivation and a slap in the face belong in a category altogether separate from bodily amputations and sexual assault.

Definitions represent the first great challenge. Some human rights activists contend that yelling at a prisoner represents the kind of "cruel, inhuman, or degrading" treatment McCain would categorically outlaw. Furthermore, some of the techniques used in the interrogation of terrorists are also used on American military personnel in the course of intensive training. Does this represent torture? Surely not.

Under certain circumstances, most morally sensitive persons would surely allow interrogators to yell at prisoners and to use psychological intimidation, sleep deprivation, and the removal of creature comforts for purposes of obtaining vital information. In increasingly serious cases, most would likely allow some use of pharmaceuticals and more intensive and manipulative psychological techniques. In the most extreme of conceivable cases, most would also allow the use of far more serious mechanisms of coercion—even what we would all agree should be labeled as torture.

In his article, Krauthammer proposes the "ticking time bomb" scenario as an example of a context in which the most serious and extreme measures would be authorized. In such a scenario, agents of the state would hold in custody a terrorist who knows where a ticking time bomb has been hidden—a bomb that will surely detonate and kill thousands of innocent persons. Under such a circumstance, Krauthammer argues, the use of extreme coercive measures would be legitimate, even necessary. The greater good of saving lives trumps the principle of state restraint.

There could exist circumstances in which such uses of torture might be made necessary.

A similar scenario may hit even closer to home for most persons. Consider the hypothetical case in which a kidnapper, now in police custody, knows where a child has been hidden in a subterranean vault with limited oxygen. He refuses to disclose the child's location, knowing that the possession of this information will serve as proof of his guilt. Time is running out and the child will soon die if the location is not found. So, what parent would not authorize the use of almost any mechanism of coercion in this case—even the most extreme? In such a case, the parent would agree with Krauthammer that the kidnapper has forfeited all claims upon psychological peace and physical comfort—even upon life itself—by refusing to save the child he has kidnapped.

Yet, even as morally serious persons might justify such actions, the use of these hypothetical scenarios is not fully satisfying. In reality, the real-life situations in which such decisions are made are rarely so clearly defined. Is this really the kidnapper? Do we really know that this captured terrorist knows where the bomb is located? Are we certain that a bomb exists?

Moral cowards duck these questions even as the morally unserious dismiss them. This is not an option for Christians who would think seriously about this urgent question. I would argue that we cannot condone torture by codifying a list of exceptional situations in which techniques of torture might be legitimately used. At the same time, I would also argue that we cannot deny that there could exist circumstances in which such uses of torture might be made necessary.

We are simply not capable ... of constructing a set of principles and rules for torture that could adequately envision the real-life scenarios.

McCain wants a categorical ban, but accepts that exceptions may, under extreme situations, be made. Krauthammer wants to define the exceptions so that a policy may be more coherent and, in his view, honest. Others, such as Harvard law professor Alan Dershowitz, suggest that specific processes be put into place that would allow for the authorization of such techniques of coercion, going so far as to suggest something like a "warrant" for torture "to be required as a precondition to the infliction of any type of torture under any circumstances."

This appears to be neither practical nor prudent, for the circumstances in which such a use of coercion might be conceived would often not allow time for such a warrant to be issued. The War on Terror is not fought on convenient terms. Furthermore, institutionalizing torture under such a procedure would almost surely lead to a continual renegotiation of the rules and constant flexing of the definitions.

We are simply not capable, I would argue, of constructing a set of principles and rules for torture that could adequately envision the real-life scenarios under which the pressure and temptation to use extreme coercion would be seriously contemplated.

Instead, I would suggest that Senator McCain is correct in arguing that a categorical ban should be adopted as state policy for the U.S., its military, and its agents. At the same time, I would admit that such a policy, like others, has limitations that, under extreme circumstances, may be transcended by other moral claims. The key point is this—at all times and in all cases the use of torture is understood to be morally suspect in the extreme, and generally unjustified.

Of course, my understanding is based in an Augustinian conception of human nature and sinfulness. At our best, we are sinners whose sin contaminates our highest aspirations and most noble actions. As Augustine argued, the Christian soldier may kill enemy combatants as a matter of true necessity, but he can never assume that in doing so he has not sinned. Augustine's "melancholy soldier" knows that the use of deadly force against another human being is, generally speaking, sin. Yet, he also knows that a failure or refusal to kill can at times be a sin worse in both intention and effect than a decision to kill in order to save lives. In a very real sense, that soldier cannot privilege his desire to be free from the sin of killing another human being to supersede his responsibility to save the lives of innocents. As philosopher Michael Walzer argues, this is the perennial problem of "dirty hands." The honest soldier knows this problem all too well—as does the interrogator.

Rules institutionalize a reality and shape a society. The safe transit of automobiles requires a set of well-established, public, and intelligible traffic laws, including speed limits. At the same time, a parent rushing a bleeding child to the hospital may be stopped by a police officer, but such a parent is not likely to be arrested and prosecuted for breaking this law. Why? Because the parent's action, under a set of unexpected but conceivable conditions, was understood by legal authorities to have been justified under this precise set of circumstances. The government does not stipulate in advance that such a set of allowable conditions exists, nor does it attempt to exhaust in advance what circumstances might exist that would be similarly justified. Instead, the law is understood to remain in full effect with full integrity even as legitimate and authorized legal agents decide not to arrest or prosecute a citizen whose law-breaking was understood to be justified under these precise circumstances. The rule is unchanged, and the law is not mocked.

We live in a fallen world threatened by agents of terror who are changing the reality of war.

Similarly, the practice of medicine involves the physician's responsibility to make split-second life and death decisions in the course of medical extremity. No precise set of laws, rules, or regulations can be set forth in advance, even as principles and best practices for medical practice are standardized. One simply cannot remove the physician as a responsible moral agent in the actual context of medical practice—even and especially in emergency cases. Yet, medical review boards exist to review the physician's decisions and actions in retrospect.

These two contexts of moral decision-making can serve to develop a coherent and principled policy on the state's use of torture and extreme coercion. First, the use of torture should be prohibited as a matter of state policy—period. No set of qualifications and exceptions can do anything but diminish the moral credibility of this policy. At the same time, rare exceptions under extreme circumstances can be considered under those circumstances by legitimate state agents, knowing that a full accounting of these decisions must be made to the public, through appropriate means and mechanisms.

Second, a thorough and legitimate review must be conducted subsequent to the use of any such techniques, with the agents who authorized or conducted such use of torture fully accountable, even to the point of maximum legal prosecution if their use of extreme coercion is seen to have been unjustified (not simply because the interrogation did not produce the desired information, but because the grounds of justification were invalid). The absence of legitimate accountability through a thorough and comprehensive process of review—with the threat of real and appropriate sanctions against those found to have acted without due justification—makes the state complicit in a web of cruelty and the official rationalization of evil.

We live in a fallen world threatened by agents of terror who are changing the reality of war and would end civilization as we know it, killing noncombatants without conscience as a matter of pride. In confronting this new form of evil, we are now forced to rethink many of the most settled questions of morality and the use of force. Nevertheless, we have no choice but to fight this foe and to wage war on those who would use mass murder and terror to sever the fragile bonds of human society. Yet, in fighting this war it is inevitable that we will look down and find dirty hands, even in doing what we would all agree is a lamentable necessity. What we must not do is compound the problem of dirty hands by adopting dirty rules.

The United States Should Not Attempt to Codify Exceptions to a Ban on Torture

Mark Bowden

Mark Bowden is a national correspondent for the magazine The Atlantic Monthly *and a best-selling author.*

The thorny issue of torture paid a visit recently to Mackenzie Allen (Geena Davis), television's newest president of the United States [a reference to a 2008 television show called *Commander in Chief*]. A terrorist plot to attack elementary schools was uncovered and a ringleader arrested, but his refusal to cooperate with interrogators placed the nation's children at terrible risk—a perfect crisis for the nation's first maternal commander in chief. Torn but principled, the rookie president instructs her staff, "I don't want to hear anything more about torture," words a hardnosed national security staffer interprets as a plea for deniability, and a green light to get tough.

Cruel treatment of prisoners is already banned. It is prohibited by military law and by America's international agreements.

Military interrogators begin torturing the captive. Meanwhile, the president launches a risky black-ops raid to a location in Lebanon, which produces intelligence that thwarts the planned attacks. Only afterwards does she learn that the same information was extracted from the captive, who is just barely alive after the torture session. Ms. Allen is so outraged when

Mark Bowden, "Always Another Way? Sometimes Cruelty and Coercion Are Necessary in Dealing with Enemy Prisoners," *The Wall Street Journal*, November 13, 2005. www.opinionjournal.com. Reprinted with permission of *The Wall Street Journal*.

she learns of it that she fires the offending security council staffer and adopts a perplexed, angry frown.

"There is always another way to get information," she says.

Wishful Thinking About Torture

Would that it were true. We like problems to have easy solutions in America, just as we like stories to have neat, happy endings. The show illustrated to me some of the wishful thinking, mythmaking and confusion that surround the difficult issues of torture, coercion and prisoner abuse, which our nation seems incapable of thinking about coherently. Sen. John McCain has tacked a provision on the annual [2005] defense budget that would ban cruel, inhuman or degrading treatment or punishment for anyone in American custody. Having been terribly abused himself as a prisoner of war in Vietnam, Sen. McCain is a national hero, and brings a heavy load of moral authority to the table. His measure ... passed the Senate, but ... [President George W. Bush threatened a veto].

One of the myths of the American soldier is that he never mistreats a captured enemy.

I don't understand why. The provision offers nothing new or even controversial. Cruel treatment of prisoners is already banned. It is prohibited by military law and by America's international agreements. American citizens are protected by the Constitution. I see no harm in reiterating our national revulsion for it, and maybe adding even a redundant layer of legal verbiage will help redress the damage done to our country by pictures from Abu Ghraib [a U.S. detention facility in Iraq] and reports of widespread prisoner abuses in Iraq and Afghanistan. One thing it will not do, sadly, is stop the abuse of prisoners.

The story line of *Commander in Chief* portrayed a classic "ticking bomb" scenario, in which a captive refuses to divulge urgent, life-saving information. Such instances do happen, but they are rare. The national debate over torture and prisoner abuse is about something different: the tendency of soldiers in a combat zone to mistreat enemy prisoners. This latter issue was brought to a head by the photographs from Abu Ghraib, depicting the grotesque treatment of Iraqi prisoners, and by reports of more severe abuses at prison camps there and in Afghanistan.

One of the myths of the American soldier is that he never mistreats a captured enemy. If our enemy dead had voices, a multitude would testify to having been summarily shot, tortured or otherwise abused in every war Americans ever fought. Some of the worst examples took place when Americans fought each other—almost 13,000 Union prisoners died of malnutrition, disease and exposure at Andersonville Prison in Sumter County, Ga. As a race, we are no worse, or better, than anyone else.

Where there are prisons there is prisoner abuse, and where there are prisons in a war zone, whether makeshift ones in the field or the established ones like Abu Ghraib, such behavior is commonplace. Abuse should be considered the default position whenever one group of men is placed under complete supervision by another.

Minimizing Abuse

Laws and rules are vitally important, but enforcing them requires good soldiers and strict, vigilant leadership. Even in an ideal situation, say, in a civilian prison in peacetime that is well-funded and well-run, and where the guards and prisoners share the same language and culture, abuse can at best be minimized.

War is the exact opposite of an ideal situation.

"Abuse has always gone on, but I think today we just hear about it more," says Lt. Col. Lewis "Bucky" Burruss, a retired special operations commander with wide experience in conflict, who wrote about his own abuse of a prisoner in his Vietnam memoir, *Mike Force.* "I've always been surprised by how well-disciplined American soldiers are, but when you have more than 100,000 armed men in the field, and they are facing a suicidal enemy who is shooting and blowing up their buddies, not to mention their own citizens, men, women and children, you are going to have anger, and you are going to have some bad soldiers, some bad leadership and some bad treatment of prisoners."

Abu Ghraib has hurt the American mission in Iraq more than any insurgent bombing or beheading.

In the vast majority of such cases, there is no justification whatsoever for breaking the rules. Apart from moral considerations, there are practical ones. In a world of digital cameras, the Internet and global telecommunications, abuses will be reported and broadcast with graphic illustrations, and deservedly or not they will color the entire war effort.

Abu Ghraib has hurt the American mission in Iraq more than any insurgent bombing or beheading. So it is terribly important that we not accept mistreatment as inevitable, and we should do everything in our power as a nation to make sure that those who break the rules are appropriately disciplined. Congress ought to pass Sen. McCain's provision and the president ought to make a great public show out of signing it. [President Bush signed the bill into law in 2005 but added a statement indicating that he reserves the right to determine interrogation limits.] But we also need to realize that prisoner abuse, like collateral damage in a bombing campaign, is one of those things that will happen whenever the country—any country—goes to war. "Atrocities follow war as the jackal follows a wounded beast," wrote John Dower, author of *War Without Mercy,* an unflinching look at racial hatred and atrocity on both sides between America and Japan in World War II.

The White House's objection to Sen. McCain's provision has little to do with Abu Ghraib or widespread prisoner abuse; it concerns the smaller piece of the torture debate, the "ticking bomb" scenario. The administration wants to protect the flexibility of the CIA [Central Intelligence Agency], and of military special ops interrogators, to coerce intelligence from rare captives like Khalid Sheikh Mohammad, chief engineer of the Sept. 11, 2001, attacks and operations chief for al Qaeda.

Prosecution and punishment remains an executive decision, and . . . there are times when coercion is demonstrably the right thing to do.

Despite the moral assurance of a television show like *Commander in Chief*, this question also has no easy answer. If there were "always another way" to get vital, potentially life-saving intelligence, as the show suggested, or if coercion always yielded bad information, cruelty would be completely unnecessary and virtue would cost nothing. We could treat all captured terrorists as honored guests without sacrificing a thing. But in certain singular instances coercion is necessary and appropriate.

The point the White House is missing here is that even with important captives like Khalid Sheikh Mohammad, official authorization for severe interrogation is not necessary. Just as there is no way to draw a clear line between coercion and torture, there is no way to define, a priori, circumstances that justify harsh treatment. Any attempt to codify it unleashes the sadists and leads to widespread abuse. Interrogators who choose coercive methods would, and should, be breaking the rules.

That does not mean that they should always be taken to task. Prosecution and punishment remains an executive decision, and just as there are legal justifications for murder, there are times when coercion is demonstrably the right thing to do.

Organizations to Contact

The editors have compiled the following list of organizations concerned with the issues debated in this book. The descriptions are derived from materials provided by the organizations. All have publications or information available for interested readers. The list was compiled on the date of publication of the present volume; the information provided here may change. Readers need to remember that many organizations take several weeks or longer to respond to inquiries.

Action by Christians Against Torture (ACAT)
8 Southfield, Saltash, Cornwall   PL12 4LX
   UK
01752 843417
e-mail: uk.acat@googlemail.com
Web site: www.acatuk.org.uk

Action by Christians Against Torture was formed in 1984 by the then British Council of Churches, with the support of Amnesty International. ACAT's mission is to work for the abolition of torture worldwide by increasing awareness among Christians of the widespread and evil use of torture and the need, for reasons of Christian faith, to campaign for its abolition. As part of this work, ACAT seeks information on specific examples of torture worldwide, advocates with governments, keeps abreast of legislation, and supports victims of torture. ACAT publishes a bimonthly newsletter on torture, available on its Web site.

Amnesty International USA (AIUSA)
5 Penn Plaza, New York, NY   10001
(212) 807-8400 • fax: (212) 627-1451
e-mail: aimember@aiusa.org
Web site: www.aiusa.org

Amnesty International is a grassroots activist organization with over 1.8 million members worldwide. Amnesty International USA is the U.S. Section of Amnesty International. The organization undertakes research and action to prevent and end grave abuses of human rights, including the rights to physical and mental integrity, freedom of conscience and expression, and freedom from discrimination. The group's Web site contains a section on human rights, with a 12-point program to prevent torture, and a search of AIUSA's Web site produces issue briefs and other materials on the subject of torture.

Center for Justice & Accountability (CJA)
870 Market St., Suite 688, San Francisco, CA 94102
(415) 544-0444 • fax: (415) 544-0456
e-mail: center4justice@cja.org
Web site: www.cja.org

The Center for Justice & Accountability is an international human rights organization dedicated to ending torture and other severe human rights abuses around the world. CJA uses litigation to hold perpetrators individually accountable for human rights abuses, develop human rights law, and advance the rule of law in countries transitioning from periods of abuse. CJA's Web site provides information for survivors, information about its cases, various publications, and links to other human rights organizations concerned with torture.

The Center for Victims of Torture (CVT)
426 C St. NE, Washington, DC 20002
(202) 548-0116 • fax: (202) 548-0118
e-mail: cvt@cvt.org
Web site: www.cvt.org

The Center for Victims of Torture is a private, nonprofit, nonpartisan organization founded to stop government-sponsored torture and heal the wounds of this torture on individuals, their families, and communities. CVT fulfills its mission in four ways: (1) by providing services directly to torture survivors; (2) by training health, education, and human services professionals who work with torture survivors; (3) by conducting research on the effects of torture and treatment methods; and (4) by advocating for public policy initiatives to help survivors and put an end to torture worldwide. CVT's Web site offers journal articles and a useful bibliography on the subject of torture.

Human Rights First

333 Seventh Ave., 13th Floor, New York, NY   10001-5108
(212) 845-5200 • fax: (212) 845-5299
e-mail: feedback@humanrightsfirst.org
Web site: www.humanrightsfirst.org

Human Rights First was founded in 1978 as the Lawyers Committee for International Human Rights to promote laws and policies that advance universal rights and freedoms. The organization exists to protect people at risk, including refugees, victims of torture or other mass human rights violations, victims of discrimination, and others. It accomplishes this mission by advocating for changes in government and international policies, seeking justice through the courts, and raising awareness and understanding through the media. The group's Web site contains links to numerous publications, many related to torture and human rights abuses. One illustrative example is "Broken Laws Broken Bodies: Torture and the Right to Redress in Indonesia."

Human Rights Watch (HRW)

1630 Connecticut Ave. NW, Suite 500
Washington, DC   20009
(202) 612-4321 • fax: (202) 612-4333
e-mail: hrwdc@hrw.org
Web site: www.hrw.org

Human Rights Watch is an independent, nongovernmental organization supported by contributions from private individuals and foundations worldwide. HRW conducts fact-finding investigations into human rights abuses and publishes those findings in dozens of books and reports. HRW also meets with government officials to urge changes in policy and practice and provides up-to-the-minute information about conflicts while they are under way. The organization's Web site contains numerous publications about torture around the world, including news articles, legislative statements, and sections entitled "Q&A: The Legal Prohibition Against Torture," "Summary of International and U.S. Law Prohibiting Torture and Other Ill-treatment of Persons in Custody," and "U.S. Torture and Abuse of Detainees."

**International Rehabilitation Council
for Torture Victims (IRCT)**
Borgergade 13, PO Box 9049 DK-1022, Copenhagen
  Denmark
+45 33 76 06 00 • fax: +45 33 76 05 00
e-mail: irct@irct.org
Web site: www.irct.org

The International Rehabilitation Council for Torture Victims is an independent, international health professional organization based in Denmark that promotes and supports the rehabilitation of torture victims and works for the prevention of torture worldwide. The group publishes *The Torture Journal*, a publication intended to provide a multidisciplinary forum for the exchange of original research and systematic reviews among professionals concerned with the biomedical, psychological, and social interface of torture. The IRCT also publishes a bimonthly electronic newsletter that focuses on issues relating to the question of torture in the context of the fight against terrorism.

Physicians for Human Rights
1156 15th St. NW, Suite 1001, Washington, DC   20005
(202) 728-5335 • fax: (202) 728-3053
Web site: http://physiciansforhumanrights.org

Physicians for Human Rights mobilizes health professionals to advance health, dignity, and justice; investigate human rights abuses and work to stop them; and promote the right to health for all. A search of the group's Web site produces a wealth of reports, press releases, and legal opinions on the topic of torture. Examples include "Striking Hard: Torture in Tibet" and "Break Them Down: Systematic Use of Psychological Torture by U.S. Forces."

REDRESS
87 Vauxhall Walk, London   SE11 5HJ
   UK
+44 (0)20 7793 1777 • fax: +44 (0)20 7793 1719
e-mail: info@redress.org
Web site: www.redress.org

REDRESS is an anti-torture advocacy organization that seeks to obtain justice for survivors of torture, to hold accountable the governments and individuals who perpetrate torture, and to develop the means of ensuring compliance with international standards and securing remedies for victims. REDRESS publications available on its Web site include various reports, the *REDRESS Newsletter, Victims' Rights Working Group Bulletin, ICC Victims' Rights Legal Update,* and the *EU Update on International Crimes.*

Survivors of Torture, International
PO Box 151240, San Diego, CA   92175
(619) 278-2400 • fax: (619) 294-9405
e-mail: survivors@notorture.org
Web site: www.notorture.org

Survivors of Torture, International, was founded in 1997 as a grassroots nonprofit agency headquartered in the home of one of its three cofounders, Kathi Anderson. The group focuses on providing services to torture survivors in the San Diego, California, area. Therapists hired by the organization assist survivors by providing psychological counseling, preparing affidavits to document the psychological effects of torture, and testifying on clients' behalf at asylum court hearings. The group's Web site provides links to numerous other torture treatment centers and human rights organizations concerned with torture issues.

United Nations Office of the High Commissioner for Human Rights (OHCHR)

Palais Wilson, 52 rue des Pâquis, Geneva   CH-1201
  Switzerland
+41 22 917 90 00
e-mail: InfoDesk@ohchr.org
Web site: www.ohchr.org

The mission of OHCHR is to work for the protection of all human rights for all people, to help empower people to realize their rights, and to assist those responsible for upholding such rights in ensuring that they are implemented. To carry out this mission, the OHCHR works with governments, legislatures, courts, national institutions, civil society, regional and international organizations, and the United Nations system. The OHCHR Web site is a source of news and events, fact sheets, and other reference materials on the issue of torture. Examples include fact sheets entitled "The International Bill of Rights," "Combating Torture," and "The Rights of the Child."

World Organisation Against Torture (OMCT)

PO Box 21, 8, rue du Vieux-Billard, Geneva 8   CH-1211
  Switzerland
+ 41 22 809 4939 • fax: + 41 22 809 4929
e-mail: omct@omct.org
Web site: www.omct.org

The World Organisation Against Torture is a coalition of international non-governmental organizations (NGOs) fighting against torture; summary executions; enforced disappearances; and all other cruel, inhuman, or degrading treatment. Based in Geneva, Switzerland, OMCT's International Secretariat provides personalized medical, legal, and/or social assistance to torture victims and fights to protect individuals and their human rights. OMCT's Web site contains links to numerous reports and publications on the issue of torture, including "Attacking the Root Causes of Torture—Poverty, Inequality, and Violence."

Bibliography

Books

Mirko Bagaric and Julie Clarke — *Torture: When the Unthinkable Is Morally Permissible.* Albany, NY: State University of New York Press, 2007.

Bob Brecher — *Torture and the Ticking Bomb.* Hoboken, NJ: Wiley-Blackwell, 2007.

Eric Stener Carlson — *The Pear Tree: Is Torture Ever Justified?* Gardena, CA: Clarity Press, 2006.

Mark Danner — *Torture and Truth: America, Abu Ghraib, and the War on Terror.* New York: New York Review of Books, 2004.

Karen J. Greenberg, Joshua L. Dratel, and Anthony Lewis, eds. — *The Torture Papers: The Road to Abu Ghraib.* New York: Cambridge University Press, 2005.

Stephen Grey — *Ghost Plane: The True Story of the CIA Torture Program.* New York: St. Martin's Press, 2006.

Lisa Hajjar — *Courting Conflict: The Israeli Military Court System in the West Bank and Gaza.* Berkeley, CA: University of California Press, 2004.

Michael Kerrigan — *The Instruments of Torture.* Guilford, CT: The Lyons Press, 2007.

Sanford Levinson   *Torture: A Collection.* New York: Oxford University Press, 2006.

Joseph Margulies   *Guantánamo and the Abuse of Presidential Power.* New York: Simon & Schuster, 2006.

Alfred McCoy   *A Question of Torture: CIA Interrogation, from the Cold War to the War on Terror.* New York: Holt Paperbacks, 2006.

Almerindo E. Ojeda   *The Trauma of Psychological Torture.* Westport, CT: Praeger Publishers, 2008.

Trevor Paglen and A.C. Thompson   *Torture Taxi: On the Trail of the CIA's Rendition Flights.* Brooklyn, NY: Melville House, 2006.

Physicians for Human Rights   *Broken Laws, Broken Lives: Medical Evidence of Torture by US Personnel and Its Impact.* Cambridge, MA: Physicians for Human Rights, June 2008.

Darius Rejali   *Torture and Democracy.* Princeton, NJ: Princeton University Press, 2007.

Philippe Sands   *Torture Team: Rumsfeld's Memo and the Betrayal of American Values.* Hampshire, UK: Palgrave Macmillan, 2008.

Periodicals

Becky Akers	"Top-Level Torture: The Bush Administration Admits to Condoning Acts That Most People Would Deem Torture," *The New American*, June 9, 2008, Vol. 24, Iss. 12, p. 25.
Stephen Armstrong	"Rough Justice," *The New Statesman*, March 19, 2007.
John Barry, Michael Hirsch, and Michael Isikoff	"The Roots of Torture," *Newsweek*, May 24, 2004.
Mark Benjamin	"The Abu Ghraib Files," *Salon*, February 16, 2006.
Michael Crawford	"Interrogation Versus Torture in the War on Terror," *MILNET.com*, 2005.
Alan M. Dershowitz	"Torture Could Be Justified," *CNN.com*, March 4, 2003.
The Economist	"Is Torture Ever Justified?" September 20, 2007.
The Economist (US)	"Tortured Truth; Abu Ghraib," May 17, 2008, Vol. 387, Iss. 8580, p. 102.
Bob Herbert	"All Too Human," *New York Times*, June 28, 2008.
Seymour M. Hersch	"Torture at Abu Ghraib," *The New Yorker*, May 10, 2004.
Paul Kramer	"The Water Cure," *The New Yorker*, February 25, 2008.

Dahlia Lithwick   "Getting Away with Torture," *Newsweek*, May 5, 2008, Vol. 151, Iss. 18, p. 17.

Jane Mayer   "The Black Sites: A Rare Look Inside the CIA's Secret Interrogation Program," *The New Yorker*, August 13, 2007.

Andrew C. McCarthy   "Torture: Thinking About the Unthinkable," *Commentary Magazine*, July 14, 2004, Vol. 118, No. 1.

The Milli Gazette Online   "'War on Terror' Threatens 'War on Torture,'" June 24, 2006.

New York Times   "Notes from the War on Terror," May 2, 2008.

New York Times   "The Torture Sessions," April 20, 2008.

The Progressive   "Torturers in the White House," June 2008, Vol. 72, Iss. 6, p. 7.

Josh Rovenger   "Analysis: Obama vs. McCain on Torture," *Citizens for Global Solutions*, May 29, 2008.

Lisa Schlein   "UN Investigator Says Torture Widespread Around Globe," *Voice of America*, March 27, 2007.

Tim Starks   "House Panel Keeps Torture Language out of Intelligence Authorization Bill," *CQ Weekly*, May 12, 2008, Vol. 66, Iss. 19, p. 1272.

Andrew Sullivan   "The Torture Tape Fingering Bush as a War Criminal," *The Sunday Times*, December 23, 2007.

Washington Post   "Legalizing Torture," June 9, 2004, p. A20.

Bob Weir   "Torture: Can We Handle the Truth?" *The American Thinker*, January 8, 2005.

Index